contents

introduction

Going to university is exciting. Whether you are a school leaver or a mature student going back to study, it can change your life and open up enormous opportunities, as well as being a great experience. So take advantage of all it has to offer and enjoy it.

But it can be hard work as well, particularly if you have to work your way through college or juggle other responsibilities at the same time. To make the most of it you need to develop life skills, such as managing your money, your time, and – above all – yourself.

Only you can keep yourself going when the going gets tough, only you can have the discipline to work when you'd rather not, and only you can take the trouble to exploit all the opportunities that are open to you. And, although there is plenty of support for you – from friends, family, partner, fellow students, tutors, university support services, not to mention books like this – only you can take advantage of them.

Develop the life skills you need and you will find that you will get much more out of your time at university. Free from worries, in control of your life, you can enjoy the present and look forward to a great future.

So make the most of your time at university!

becoming a student

Becoming a student will change your life, whether you are a school leaver or a mature student returning to study after a period of work or bringing up children. As a student you will face new challenges and meet new people, some of whom may become lifelong friends. You can expect to be stretched as you prepare for a career, or change of career.

You will learn not only about the subject you are studying, but also about yourself and what you can make of the rest of your life. You will develop a new way of looking at the world which will stay with you whatever you do afterwards. You will be a different person by the time you leave.

So it is only natural to feel a bit anxious as well as eager and excited about going to university. The chances are that most other people will be feeling like that too.

But don't worry – during freshers' week you will have the chance to settle in, find your way around, and meet lots of people. Join a few clubs and societies, don't be afraid to make the first move, and be ready to join in.

Take it easy, though. You don't have to do everything – you won't have time once your course has got under way – and you don't have to be friends for life with the people you meet in the first few weeks.

And in a very short time university will feel like home and you will have found the people you really want to be friends with.

School leavers

If you are a school or college leaver, you may be living away from home for the first time. Even if you are living in hall for the first year, you will have more freedom than you have ever had before: freedom to live your own life, to do well and have a good time; but also the freedom to mess up.

 ## Managing your time

The big difference between school and university is that at university you will be treated as an adult. Nobody will be waking you up on time to get to lectures – you will have to take responsibility for getting there yourself. If you miss lectures you will have to make up the work somehow, and if you miss too many you may face a penalty, such as losing marks.

One of the major differences you will notice is that you are likely to be working to much longer timescales than you did at school. If you are lucky you may find that pieces of work come in a steady trickle at first so that you have time to get used to this. If so, don't be lulled into a false sense of security. You will soon be given assignments further ahead.

Don't expect your tutors to balance out your work for you – if you get several assignments that have to be to be handed in at the same time, it is up to you to manage your time. This means that you have to think and plan ahead, because if you don't, sooner or later you will find yourself overwhelmed by the amount of work you have to do. Doing the work in a rush or by staying up all night is not the best way to get good grades.

 ## Academic work

Expect to read much more widely than before. This is one of the factors that makes the difference between an OK assignment and a good one. It is up to you to see that you get hold of the books you need. You certainly won't be able to buy them all, so you will need to get to the library early or you will find that the books you want are already out on loan.

Make sure you know what is expected of you with each piece of work. If it isn't clear what the tutor is expecting, ask. The tutor may think it is obvious. That doesn't matter. The only way that you will get a good grade is by knowing what the tutor wants – and tutors may have different ideas about what makes a good assignment. It is up to you to find out what each tutor wants and to produce it.

 ## Managing money

You will already have arranged your loan or grant. You will also need a bank. Banks fall over themselves to attract students because most people stick with the same bank all their lives. Graduates tend to earn more money than non-graduates, so they are regarded as good customers.

Take the longer view, ignore the freebies and look at the service the banks are offering you as a student. Look for the best deals on overdrafts. Some banks may give you free overdraft facilities up to a certain amount. Check how much interest you will be paying above that level. Find out how long you will have to pay off any debts after leaving university. Wise up.

When you get your loan or grant, you may find that you have more money than you have ever dreamt of. Be warned – it won't last. If you don't budget carefully you will find that your overdraft gets out of control and you will be getting nasty letters from the bank. Learn to manage money and sleep easy.

 ## Looking after yourself

If you are living away from home for the first time, you will have to get used to the fact that nobody will be there to make your breakfast or wash your clothes. If you are catering for yourself, there will be no-one to do the shopping for you either. Get organised.

Equally, nobody will be checking what time you come in at night. Most people enjoy their freedom at university and most people do some silly things from time to time. Drink, drugs and sex may be freely available but make sure you are not taking undue risks with your health.

Remember to register with a doctor. You may not expect to get ill and you probably won't, but don't create a problem for yourself. The university will probably suggest who you should register with.

Mature students

Being a student

If you are a mature student, you are likely to be living at home. In this respect the change of lifestyle may seem less extreme than for school leavers. Yet you are taking on a whole new identity – that of a student. You may associate students with an entirely different lifestyle from your own. This is a great opportunity to extend your horizons, and you may find that you get more out of it if you think through the differences beforehand.

You may have worked for a few years and in the process acquired some knowledge of the wider world and some self-discipline. You may feel this creates a gulf between you and the school leavers who are probably in the majority in your group. Or you may be thrilled at the chance to let go for a bit. Think about how much you want to change your lifestyle and in what way.

If you are bringing up children you will be used to taking responsibility for others, yet you may find that you are treated as someone who needs to be told what to do. The other students could be the same age as your own children.

You will have to think about how you will get on with them. Do you want to socialise with them or will you have to go straight home after lectures?

You will stand in a different relationship to the other adults, the tutors. You may be older than some of them, yet they will be in a position of authority over you. Do you feel OK with this? And how will you relate to them?

You may also have the problem that your partner, family or friends don't have the experience of going to university and may not underst and your need for time to study or read quietly. Talk to them about what is involved and tell them how they can help you. If you have the wholehearted support of those nearest to you, it will make your life a lot easier.

 ## Managing money

Your financial situation will probably change as a result of being a student. You may have had to give up a job to study, or take a less well-paid part-time job. You will find books an expensive extra. If you are used to a certain lifestyle you may find it hard to change at first. If you didn't have much money in the first place and going to university has been a struggle, you may have to watch your expenditure even more carefully. How will you feel about having less money and having to budget? What are you happy to cut down on?

 ## Managing your time

Experience will probably have taught you how to manage time, whether this means getting to work on time, getting children to school on time, or working to deadlines. If so, you will find that you have an advantage over younger students. But, like them, you may have to learn to manage longer timescales. You can expect to be given assignments well in advance and you will be expected to manage your time yourself.

If you have family or other commitments, you will have to juggle your priorities. If you have children who need to be picked up from school, how will you manage if this clashes with lectures? What will you do if one of the children is sick? Make sure that you have contingency plans in place, so that you don't have to worry too much about what might go wrong. If there are other mature students on your course, you may be able to arrange to get copies of handouts for each other if any of you has to miss a lecture.

Academic work

If you haven't studied for a while, you may be worried about your ability to take notes and write essays. Many universities now run courses on study skills, so take advantage of whatever is on offer. There are also plenty of books on the subject and most university libraries will have some.

If it is a long time since you studied, you may find teaching methods have changed. Expect to find a wider range of methods and to take an active part in class. Give yourself time to settle in and adjust. You will soon get into the swing of it. You may find that active learning methods such as discussion groups are easier for you than for the younger students, because you have more life experience to draw on and are more used to speaking up in front of others.

The 5 keys to success as a student

- *take control of your own life – now*
- *know what you want*
- *be realistic*
- *look ahead*
- *be flexible.*

The keys to success

Take control of your life

Deciding to go to university is probably one of the most important decisions you have ever made. If you are a school leaver, it is probably the first major decision you have taken for yourself. If you are a mature student, it may be a major change of direction for you, and it may require sacrifices.

Either way, it is important to make the most of your opportunities. To do this you need to take control of your own life. The opposite is to drift, to take the easy option, and to feel dissatisfied as a result. You can't go back in time if, after you've left university, you wished you'd done things differently.

"Life is not a rehearsal"

Imagine driving down a road, not knowing where you are going. You won't know whether to take this turning or that. It probably won't matter much. As you don't know where you are going, you don't know if you are going the right way, or when you will get there, if at all.

You might be happy just driving along, taking the easiest route, or the one that looked most interesting at the time. You might like the place you end up in or you might hate it. But when you finally decide where you want to go, you could find yourself miles off track. And you could spend a long time trying to get back to where you wanted to be. This can be frustrating and expensive.

 ## Know what you want

Knowing what you want is the first step to getting it. Spend a little time getting as clear as you can about this. If you want to change your life in some way, think about what changing your life would mean.

If you want a specific career find out what you have to do, whether it is the class of degree you have to get, or what kind of opportunities might be open to you. Don't wait until you've missed your chances. Even if time is short, making time to find out will save you time in the long run.

Be realistic

Work out what you can reasonably do and what you can aim at. To continue the metaphor, don't aim at driving 600 miles if you only have fuel for 400. See what there is within a 400-mile radius that you would like. Think about what is practicable in your own circumstances.

Look ahead

You are where you are today because of what you did yesterday. The way you spent your time, the people you spent it with, the things you learnt to care about, all contributed to the decisions you made that have led you to being where you are today. Tomorrow will be the way it is because of what you do today. Where you put your effort and attention will shape your tomorrows.

"Today is yesterday's tomorrow."

If you take pains with your academic work, you will get better grades. If you take the trouble to find out early about possible career prospects and prepare for the future, you will find that what you have done at university supports your chosen career path. This may seem like a long way off, but decisions taken in the first and second years may either support your career choices or narrow them.

Be flexible

On your journey, you may find new avenues opening up, or you may find road blocks barring your way. Keep in mind the direction in which you want to go, and if circumstances change, look to see how a different route might get you to where you want to be – or something like it.

The urgent versus the important

One of the most important lessons you can learn in life is the difference between the urgent and the important. Getting an idea of where you are going is important. It may not be urgent in the sense that there is a deadline for doing it. If you leave it a while it will still be there waiting to be done.

If something is urgent it means that you have a deadline, and if you miss that deadline it's too late to do anything about it. Some people spend their lives only doing the urgent. They never do the really important things, like thinking about what they want and preparing for the future, because there isn't a deadline. This is like driving along, filling up the car with petrol, getting it serviced, stopping at red lights – but never consulting the map or planning a route. Get to know the difference between the urgent and the important and you will get in control of your life.

Another way of looking at it is to use the grid below. Stop and think for a moment about some of the things you have to do. Which box would you put them in? For example, deciding about next year's options if you have a deadline approaching would be in box 1 – high urgency and high importance. Finishing an assignment that is due in would also be in box 1, and so would seeing a friend who is in trouble.

Deciding on your future career at the moment is probably box 2 – high importance, low urgency – since the deadline for any decision is some way off. Some social things can go in this box. For instance, it's important that you meet up with your friends, but it isn't usually urgent – you can always do it another time.

Box 3 (high urgency, low importance) is for anything that doesn't matter too much to you, but if you're going to do it, you have to do it now. An example would be going to a match or a gig you'd quite like to go to but don't mind too much if you miss it.

Box 4 is for things that are low urgency and low importance. They are often time wasters: for example, I sometimes find myself killing time playing computer games. It isn't important to me or particularly enjoyable and it certainly isn't urgent.

	High importance	Low importance
High urgency	1	3
Low urgency	2	4

Make a short list of some of the things you have to do, or intend to do. Which boxes do they fit into? Your ideas about what is important may well be different from mine, so put down what you really think.

If you find that most of the things on your list fall into boxes 3 and 4, maybe you should start thinking about what is important in your life. If too many things fall into box 4, you aren't making the most of your opportunities. And if box 2 is empty, it is time to think about your priorities.

Remember, this is your life and nobody else's. What you make of it is up to you.

chapter 2

getting motivated and staying motivated

At university there is only one person who will take responsibility for your life – you. No-one else is going to do it. If you are a mature student you are probably well aware of this, but even so, you may not have taken as much responsibility for your own work as you do at university.

To do this successfully, you need to learn how to motivate yourself. This is a real skill and one that will stand you in good stead for the rest of your life. It is easy to stay on track when things are going well, but when the work becomes hard, or parts of the course are boring, or you have problems or other distractions – that is when you need motivation skills.

One of the reasons we become demotivated is because experiences do not live up to our expectations. Often we do not examine our expectations, and sometimes we are not aware that we have any. But whether you are a school leaver or a mature student you will probably have some expectations of what university will be like, or you would not have chosen to go.

People's expectations are usually based on their own previous educational experiences or on those of family or friends. This means that not everybody has the same expectations, because the type of education on offer varies from school to school and changes over the years. So if a group of students were asked what they expected from university, although there would be some common strands, there would also be some differences.

Mature students might be thinking back to their own schooling ten or 20 years ago, which may have been different from how it is now. School leavers might expect university to be much the same as school, but with the opportunity to live as they please. Overseas students might have had a very different experience of education from the British experience, and have that as the basis of their expectations. Some people may have heard about the experiences of older brothers or sisters or parents when they were at university and think it will be the same.

It is almost certain that unless you know someone who has been to university recently and has been to a similar type of university as yours, your expectations will be different from reality. Of course, your expectations may be exceeded. Or you may come down to earth with a bump. You may feel disillusioned in some way. Exploring some of your expectations at an early stage will help you deal with these feelings, become more open to what you will actually experience as a student, and enable you to make the most of it instead of wishing something was different.

Some of the most important expectations concern the way in which you are taught, the relationships with lecturers and tutors, and how hard you will have to work. Take a few moments to think about the questions opposite. Write down your answers and be as specific as you can, then compare them with the discussion below.

Expectations of teaching and learning

Discussion

Question 1

Teaching and learning methods will vary a lot depending on the type of university you are at and the course you are on, so there are no 'right' answers to the questions. However, in general, you can expect to spend a substantial amount of time in private study or working with other people without the teacher.

Exercise

Expectations of teaching and learning

1. How much information do you expect to be given by your teachers in class and how much do you expect to read up and acquire for yourself?

2. What kind of teaching and learning methods do you expect?

3. How much direction do you expect to get on how to do an assignment?

4. Do you expect to develop your own ideas or to follow what your teachers tell you?

5. Do you expect all the subjects you take to be taught in much the same way?

If you are not sure how much time you should be spending on this, look through your course literature, or ask your tutors. Even better, ask a successful second- or third-year student how much time they think you need to spend. If your course is based on continuous assessment (i.e. if all your assignments count towards your degree), expect to be under pressure. You will have frequent deadlines.

 ## Question 2

You can expect to encounter a variety of teaching and learning methods, although some universities are more traditional than others. If you are a mature student whose previous experience of education involved lots of note-taking and essay-writing, you may need to adjust to other methods, such as projects, group work, oral presentations, discussions and report writing. If you have had some work experience you may find that this will stand you in good stead.

 ## Question 3

You will probably find that you get less direction than you have had before, although many universities now run study skills courses or sessions in which students are given guidance on how to set about assignments and how to present their work. Even if you think you know how to study, it is worth taking advantage of them to discover some approaches that are different from the way you have done things before. Be tolerant if you hear things you already know – they may be new to some people in your group.

 ## Question 4

The extent to which you will be expected to follow your own ideas will vary with the course. Some subjects are more factual than others. Whatever you are doing, you should expect to approach the material in a critical way and be able to apply your knowledge to different situations. Sometimes students think that there is a 'right' answer. For most subjects there are theories and arguments, some of which explain the facts better than others. Learning how to make a good argument is an important skill.

 ## Question 5

You may find different subjects taught in quite different ways. This is most likely to be true if you are doing a modular course or combined studies.

If you found your answers were very different from those in the discussions above, it doesn't mean that you are wrong: universities vary in their approach. The discussion is there to help you to think about the possible differences between your expectations and what generally goes on.

 ## *Relationships with lecturers*

Another area where students' expectations are often very different from reality is the relationship they have with their lecturers. Write down your answers to the questions in the next exercise before reading on.

1. What do you think university teachers see as their main role?

2. How much responsibility do you think they should take for you and your problems?

3. What do you expect to do for yourself?

 Discussion

 Question 1

You may have answered 'teaching' to the first question. It may come as a surprise that some university teachers see themselves as researchers first and teachers second. In recent years there has been a great deal of pressure from the government for all universities to carry out research. Funding is tied to research, so a university that does not do well in the research stakes can suffer financially.

Of course, teaching is still one of the most important activities that universities undertake. And most universities believe that doing research makes lecturers into better teachers, because they are at the cutting edge of their subject. So you can gain from this.

 Question 2

Teachers will differ in the extent to which they are concerned with your life. Some may see their role simply as lecturers and assessors of your work and will not expect to be involved with you beyond that.

However, in your first year you will probably have a personal tutor who will see you from time to time to see how you are getting on, or who you can go to with any personal or academic problems. The arrangements for the second and third years may be different, but in practice you will usually find there is a tutor you can approach with any problems.

Question 3

If you have a problem it is up to you to approach your personal tutor or any other tutor you feel you can talk to. Don't expect them to be watching over you. Be aware that if you approach someone after a lecture, they may have another lecture or a meeting to go to immediately afterwards. Be prepared to raise the matter and make an appointment to see them later. And then keep the appointment.

Hopes and fears

We all have hopes and fears when we start any new venture, whether it is a new job, a new project or a new course. Our hopes motivate us and our fears demotivate us. Acknowledging what they are is the first step to realising the hopes and overcoming the fears.

Exercise

Hopes and fears

I hope that my course will enable me to . . .

What is <u>really</u> important to me about doing the course is . . .

What I <u>really</u> want while on the course is . . .

What I wouldn't like to happen is . . .

What I am most afraid of is . . .

Before you read on, complete the sentences in the box below.

Perhaps this is the first time you have thought so explicitly about what you feel and what you want from your course.

You may have found that your answers to the second and third questions were different from the first one. They may even have surprised you.

And notice how you felt when you answered the last two questions. Most of the things we fear never happen. The majority of students cope with their studies, make friends and enjoy student life. Remember, it is likely that there will be many people in the same situation as you, with similar fears.

"96% of students think that going to university is a worthwhile experience."

Mori Student Living Report 2003

Usually fear is caused by the unknown – and you will quickly get to know other people, find your way around and find out what is expected of you. If you are not sure, ask. Be prepared to take the initiative. If you have a special problem, find out what support is available as soon as possible.

Sometimes our hopes are equally unrealistic. We expect a change in circumstance to change our lives for us, and pin too much on it. This can be true for the school leaver looking forward to the freedoms that living away from home for the first time brings, and for the mature student looking for a life change, or the student from overseas looking for a different learning experience.

Your experience at university will change you. It will encourage you to think more, acquire the confidence of your own opinions, enable you to hold your own in debate and open doors to a range of satisfying careers. But these changes do not happen overnight – they are the result of the effort you make over time. There will be good days and bad days, problems as well as enjoyment. Be prepared for both.

Knowing what motivates you

Knowing what motivates you gives you a sense of purpose. It doesn't matter whether you are motivated by the thought of a good job as an accountant at the end of your course, or whether you want to find out what you are capable of, or simply want to enjoy student life. What is important is knowing what you want from the experience – and getting it. The clearer you are about the underlying reasons for doing the course, the clearer you will be about where you need to put your energy, time, and effort at university.

Think for a moment about your answers to the questions about your hopes for university life. Does the way you spend your time help you to realise those hopes? Are you hoping to get good grades, but squandering time on things you don't even especially enjoy instead of working to improve your grades? Are you hoping to have an active social life, but never joining in and never making the first move? Think about how you can match the way you spend your time to achieving your hopes.

Exercise

Complete the following sentences:

I really want . . .

The way to get this is to . . .

What stopped me from doing this in the past was . . .

From now on I am going to . . .

Knowing what you want will help when you have problems. Parts of the course may seem hard or less interesting to you. You may feel pressurised because you have to juggle study, paid work and family commitments. You may be experiencing relationship difficulties or money worries. There will be times when what you want seems far away and far removed from what you are doing, and you begin to wonder why you are here.

If that happens, think about what motivated you to do the course in the first place. Is it still important to you? If you could have that, would it make everything worthwhile? If the answer is yes, if you feel the old enthusiasm coming back, then keep that image in your mind. Revisit it when the going gets tough. If what you really want is a great job at the end of it, find out more about it, collect some information, go to talks, discuss it with people who know about it. Make it real for you.

Maybe what you want is to be able to enjoy the student experience. What do you *really* enjoy about being a student? Set aside some time for it, whether it is going clubbing all night or reading a book that has nothing to do with your assignment. Most people get the experience of being a student only once in their lives. So make the most of it. Keep a balance between the things you have to do to succeed and keep your life on track, and the things you do for pure enjoyment. All play and no work will get you nowhere. All work and no play makes for a dull life.

Of course it often happens that students change their ideas about what they want as they go through university. If you are a school leaver, this is a natural part of growing up. If you have come back to study after a break it is part of the process of development. So revisit these questions from time to time and see how your answers have changed.

Knowing how to motivate yourself

There are going to be times when whatever you have to do – whether it is getting up on time after a late night, or going on working when you feel that your brain is burning and you can't do any more – seems just too much. You think: if I don't finish this assignment now I could slip a grade. Or you think: I have to turn up or I'll get the sack from my job and I can't afford that.

To find out how you usually set about motivating yourself, think about a time when you were pushing yourself to do something. How did you do it? This may seem like a strange question to start with. Even if it was only getting up on time, think of a *specific* occasion and relive what went on inside your head. Do it now and come up with some answers before reading on.

Negative ways of motivating yourself

Sometimes people try to motivate themselves in a purely negative way. They tell themselves off and call themselves stupid or idle. They tell themselves they are no good: 'You can't get up in the morning, you keep being late, you're a failure – you can't keep a job, you get lousy grades and you'll never get anywhere,' they say to themselves. If you catch yourself having a lot of negative thoughts like this – and unless another voice kicks in immediately saying, 'Oh no, I'm not, I'll show you,' – then STOP NOW. Very few people are motivated by being put down.

Become aware of what is going through your head. Perhaps you have never thought of this before, but most of us have an internal dialogue going on during the day.

Remember it's your head, your brain and your voice. So every time you catch yourself saying something negative to yourself, say something positive instead. If the negative voice is hard to get rid of, imagine someone saying those negative things in a Donald Duck voice. Somehow, that way it doesn't sound so meaningful. Play around with it and have some fun.

Sometimes people have a daydream. They imagine what will happen, for instance, if they don't get up and go to work. They see the manager saying, 'That's the third time you've come in late this month. You're fired! Get your things and go!'

And then they see themselves not being able to pay the rent or not being able to go out for weeks until they have got another job. They imagine the hassle of getting another job and getting used to a new routine just when a really important assignment is due. They see it all in their mind's eye and feel really stressed out. Compared with getting up – now – this scenario is really bad. They get up in a rush feeling bad about themselves and make it to the job just in time. It's not a good day.

This way of motivating yourself does work for some people. They terrify themselves into doing something. The more awful the prospect of not doing what they should be doing, the more motivated they are to do it. However, if you use this method regularly you are going to spend a lot of your life imagining dreadful things happening to you. Is this really what you want to do?

 ## Positive ways of motivating yourself

The opposite method – thinking about how good it will be when you've done something – works for most people. Instead of imagining yourself getting the sack, imagine getting to work on time, feeling pleased with yourself and having a good day. Tell yourself you can do it and keep thinking positively.

Sometimes people combine the two methods, in effect saying to themselves: 'I could *either* stay in bed till I am late for work, get the sack, have a lot of hassle finding another job just when I need the time to concentrate on a really important assignment, *or* I could get up now, have a good day at work and have plenty of time for the assignment and get a really good grade.' This contrast may work for you.

Top tips for motivating yourself

* *keep reminding yourself of why you are doing it*

* *think positively*

* *make a realistic plan and stick to it*

* *take breaks*

* *give yourself rewards.*

Another way of motivating yourself, when you are starting an assignment or doing revision for instance, is to break down a large job into manageable chunks. Make a plan. Be realistic. Nothing is more demotivating than making a grand plan and finding you can't stick to it. Give yourself adequate breaks, otherwise you will find you spend more and more time achieving less and less.

Reward yourself. Switch off completely and do something you enjoy. When you come back to the task you will find that you are refreshed and ready to begin again.

And above all, remind yourself of what you will gain by doing what you've set out to do. Keep it in your mind.

 ## Finding your own ways of motivating yourself

Sometimes the best way of motivating yourself is to devise your own method. If you are not sure what that might be, think about how you would motivate a friend. What would you say or do? Would that work for you? How can you put it into practice?

Think about a time when you felt really motivated to do something, even though it was quite a challenge. Think about how you were feeling, what you were thinking, who you were with, what was going on. What was it about the situation that made you feel motivated?

The answer could be that someone had challenged you and you were set on proving yourself, or that you were working with other people in the same boat and you were helping each other. Or maybe it was because you really wanted to be able to do something and really believed that you could.

Your answers may be quite different, but the more you think about it, the more you will begin to understand what motivates you to do something, and you can begin to create those conditions for yourself.

 ## If you still feel demotivated

If you have tried to motivate yourself and you feel that everything is a constant struggle, now is the time to take a step back and find out what's wrong. Although it's good to be able to ride over the rough patches in life, if the whole of your life feels like a rough patch then you need to do some serious thinking and make some changes. Take some quiet time out and do some work on the *Points to ponder* (left).

Thinking about these things will probably be painful. But as you do so you will probably have one of two reactions – either an intense feeling that you don't want to give up or a feeling of immense relief. Let those feelings guide you. If you really are on the wrong path it is best to find out sooner rather than later.

Pinpoint the problems and start thinking about your options. If the problems are academic, talk to your tutors. If they relate to your future, talk to your careers adviser. If you have personal or financial problems, talk to your personal tutor, a student counsellor or welfare officer, or ring the students' helpline. (Information about all these services will be in your university handbook. See Chapter 10 for more details.)

You will find that tutors and counsellors have dealt with these problems before. Knowing that you are not the only person to have problems is often a relief in itself. You will probably find that problems that seem to be insuperable can in fact be resolved or lessened.

Points to ponder

- When you think about what led you to do the course does it still excite you?

- Will the course you are on help you to attain your goals?

- Are there other ways of achieving them?

- What do you really want now?

- How can you achieve it?

- What would you do if you changed to another course or dropped out?

coping with criticism

Why being able to cope with criticism is important

We all get criticised throughout our lives – by family, friends, partners, by people we like and by people we don't. Sometimes the criticism is helpful and sometimes it is hurtful.

At university you get criticism of your work. The tutor writes comments on your assignment explaining why your work has been given the grade it has and suggesting ways of improving next time.

If you have done well, reading the comments is a positive experience. But if you are feeling anxious, or are finding the work difficult, reading something that tells you what is wrong with what you have done can be demoralising and demotivating. So some students look at the grade and, if they have at least passed, never read the comments.

This isn't a good idea, as the purpose of the comments is to help you improve your work, and if you don't read them, you will continue to make the same mistakes. Your tutors will probably get exasperated if you don't take their advice on board. On the other hand, if you read the comments and apply them in the next essay you write, you may get a better grade and more positive feedback as a result.

Vicious circles and virtuous spirals

So why do we ignore advice of this kind? What happens is that we hear or read something negative about ourselves and feel bad about it. We then avoid whatever has made us feel bad – we don't read it, or we walk away, or we put it out of our minds. We continue our existing behaviour and continue to get the same negative feedback. The more certain we are that the feedback will be negative, the more strongly we avoid it.

We may even begin to dislike the task, spend less time on it, or feel too stressed to do our best. If this happens we get into a downward spiral. Our work actually gets worse and the feedback becomes more negative. Sometimes people begin to put off doing the work because it begins to be associated with something unpleasant.

> *"If God had meant today to be perfect he wouldn't have invented tomorrow."*

On the other hand, when you hear something good about yourself ('excellent piece of work') you feel good. If you get a really positive comment about an assignment, you may want to re-read it and dwell on it. The more you think about the praise, the better you feel, and the more determined you are to do your very best work next time. You're keen to start your next assignment, and work hard to do as well as before, or even better.

If your tutor has suggested some improvement, you feel inspired to tackle it. You check your work through carefully at the end so that you don't lose marks by making silly mistakes. When your work comes back you're eager to read what your tutor has written about it. If there are any more suggestions for improvement you feel quite pleased. Your work gets better and better!

How to get into a virtuous spiral

To get into that all-important virtuous spiral, think how it would be if your tutor had written the comments on your work with a view to helping you improve. Believe me, this is true: your tutor *does* want you to improve your work. Anybody who has a pile of scripts to mark is hoping that they will be well-written and interesting.

It is true even when the comments have been written hastily and without due appreciation of the feelings you might have as you read it. Nothing would please your tutor more than receiving a better assignment next time, and one in which you have worked on the areas they suggest.

If you believed your tutor really wanted you to improve, how would that change your reaction? You would probably want to make sure you understood what you had to do to improve next time and would do your best to do it.

Sometimes the problem is to do with our state of mind when we receive feedback. Without really acknowledging it to ourselves, we are either looking for praise to bolster ourselves up, or have convinced ourselves that we are going to get unfair criticism. We interpret what is written according to our needs or pre-set expectations, instead of reading them neutrally.

So, if you have a good friend who wouldn't mind exchanging assignments with you and whose work is at roughly the same level as yours, try this experiment. When your assignments come back, swap them with your friend

"Nobody can make you feel inferior without your permission."

Eleanor Roosevelt

and read each other's comments. How do you feel reading the comments about someone else's work? The chances are that you will feel that the comments are fairly factual. You don't feel downcast by what is written even when the tutor is pointing out what's wrong with the work.

Why is this? When we read criticism about something we have written, we tend to take it to heart. We receive it as if it were a criticism of our very being, not about something we are learning to do and will eventually do better.

When we read criticism of someone else's work we only read the words and receive it neutrally. Suppose you ask your friend to tell you how the tutor wants you to improve your work, and she tells you, 'Oh, he says you need to re-read your work before you hand it in because some of the sentences aren't very clear.' You will probably ask 'Where?' and if your friend reads what you have written she will probably be able to spot the sentences the tutor referred to. If she asks you what you meant when you wrote it, you can probably explain in simple language. Write down what you have just said and tidy it up a bit so that it looks like written English. This is likely to be closer to what your tutor was looking for. You have improved already!

"You are not your behaviour."

Of course, you may not want to do this exercise at all. Showing someone else what the tutor has written about your work may be the last thing you want to do. So if you want to 'go it alone', here are some ways in which you can set about it.

First of all, stop taking it personally. Distance yourself from your work. What you do or write is not the same thing as who you are. We all do stupid things sometimes and we all have off days and we all find some things are a struggle. This doesn't mean we are no good as people. But sometimes we need to change what we do.

If you learn a sport you expect to be told how to do it better by a coach or trainer. They watch what you are doing and show you how to improve your technique. Learning how to write a good assignment is a bit like that – your tutor acts as the coach and explains how you can improve.

Start with the thought that the comments will help you to get a better grade. Distance yourself from the piece of work. Imagine someone else had written it. Ask yourself what that person would have to do to improve their work next time.

Read the comments. Make a plan. If someone were told, say, that what they had written wasn't always clear, what would you suggest they did about it? Take the comments and imagine you are advising someone else. How should they tackle their assignments next time to get a better grade and more favourable feedback? Do it. Work on one or two things at a time. Ask the tutor for feedback next time on what you have been working on.

Sometimes people think they haven't got enough time to do this. However the more you work at it, the easier it gets and the less time you will need to spend on it in future. Think of anything you have learned to do in the past few years. How difficult was it to do in the first place and how long did it take you, compared with now?

Giving and receiving feedback

You may find that you have to give feedback to your fellow students, for example during an oral presentation or as part of a group project. You may be given instructions on how to do this. If not, follow these simple guidelines.

First of all, agree on the criteria you will be using, and be specific. If you are giving feedback on a presentation, think about what you might be looking for. This will, of course, depend on what the presentation is about and how skilled you all are at doing it. Structure, giving examples, making eye contact with the audience, using audiovisual aids correctly might all be criteria. Make sure everyone has the same understanding of the terms used.

Have a list of criteria in front of you and make notes if you need to. When you are watching the person give the presentation, remember that you are giving feedback on the *performance, not the person*. Whether it is your best mate or someone you loathe doesn't matter. Look objectively at what they are doing. Comparing one person with another will help. Look at what they do well, as well as what they need to work on.

When you give feedback, be positive. Start by telling them what you thought they did best. Let them have a moment to register what you have said, and then tell them what they need to work on. You can say something like 'To improve your presentation next time ...' or, 'To make your presentation even better next time, you could ...'

Top tips on giving feedback

• *be objective*

• *start with the positive*

• *be specific*

• *do it in a constructive state of mind.*

The person may want to ask you what you mean, or try to defend themselves. Stay positive. You can say, for instance, 'Next time, look up at the audience from time to time – it will make a big difference to the way the presentation is received.' *Don't* say, 'It's really boring when you read it all out like that.' Remember that your turn will come next! Think what *you* would find helpful and constructive.

If the person to whom you're giving feedback has made such a poor job of it that you find it difficult to say anything positive, start by asking them how they think they did. They probably know they made a bad job of it. Let them criticise themselves first. Then follow up with some good advice. Focus on what they have drawn attention to and only give them as much advice as you think they can handle. Or ask them what they would do differently next time.

One good way to remain constructive throughout is to get into a positive mindset before you start. Think about helping the person to improve, because if you're just going through the motions, your body language will be at odds with the words you are using, and the other person will know.

Strange as it may sound, you can tell the way someone is feeling about you even when you can't see them. People have experimented by getting a group of people to stand behind one other person and think either bad thoughts or good thoughts about the person in front. The person in front can usually tell which it is. It's like walking into a room and sensing an atmosphere.

When it's your turn to receive feedback, remember that the whole point of it is to help you do better next time. Knowing what to work on is the first step. If someone tells you, for instance, that your presentation will improve if you practise using audiovisual aids, say, 'thank you'. Don't immediately start telling them how you meant to, but you were running late with an assignment and didn't have time.

If you don't understand what they tell you, ask them to show you or explain more fully what you should do next time. Then do it!

Dealing with personal criticism

When people make personal criticisms it can be hurtful. Sometimes we take it too seriously and brood on it. After all, we all have faults and we all make mistakes. It is part of the human condition. Learning to know yourself, warts and all, and being able to accept yourself is an important lesson in life.

There may be times when you know that the criticism is justified and comes from someone well disposed towards you. Instead of being defensive, take it as a wake-up call that you need to change your behaviour. Think about what they have said. Why do you do what you do, and how can you catch yourself next time so that you don't keep doing it? What can you do instead?

Of course, sometimes people make criticisms that aren't justified. They may repeat gossip, make thoughtless remarks, or be deliberately malicious. Sometimes people do it as a way of getting a laugh or because they like putting other people down.

If you think it was thoughtlessness, talk to the person in private. Remember that your problem is with the *behaviour*, not the person. *Don't* say, 'you made me feel dreadful when you said that', as it will only put them on the defensive. Instead, explain calmly how you felt. Tell them you know they didn't mean to upset you or create trouble for you. You will probably find they are only too ready to apologise, and won't do it again.

If someone is deliberately causing trouble, they are probably a bully. They like putting other people down and seeing them suffer. The more upset you become the more they will do it. If you react differently, or if you tackle them directly, they will probably stop. The first task is to put yourself back in control. Try the following exercises and see what works for you.

Exercises

1. If someone is being unpleasant to you, distance yourself from what is going on. Imagine you can stand back and watch yourself and the other person in the situation. Notice what happens – what triggers the incident, and why it is getting to you. You may find that this in itself is enough to change the situation, because while you are observing you don't react in the same way.

2. Decide in advance how you want to deal with the situation in future. Go over in your mind what you will say and do and how you will feel about it. Keep repeating it until it becomes second nature.

3. If you find that even seeing someone makes you feel uncomfortable, try this. Imagine the person in some totally ridiculous situation, the more extreme the better. Build up the details – enjoy yourself. Imagine it larger than life and in technicolour. Next time you see the person concerned, remember that image you had of them. It will probably come to mind automatically. It will be impossible for you to react the way you did in the past.

I was once subjected to bullying at work and used the third technique listed above. Next time I saw the person concerned I remembered my picture of them. It was impossible to feel cowed with that picture in my mind. The situation became less tense because I wasn't reacting in the old way. It is very hard to bully someone who isn't responding.

But remember – if you are being bullied and these self-help techniques don't resolve the situation, tell someone: either your tutor or a student counsellor. Don't let them get away with it, as you might not be the only one they are harming.

about time

This chapter explains:

- **why it is important to manage your time effectively**
- **how our brains understand time**
- **how to plan so that you make the most of your time**
- **how to beat procrastination.**

It is important to manage your own time at university because you will be given assignments well in advance and expected to work out your own timetable for doing them. If you are on a course that involves continuous assessment you may lose marks for handing in work late. Even mature students may find they need to adjust to the long timescales.

If you have to work during term-time or have children or other people to look after, you will be under a lot of time pressure. If you are in the happy position of only having your studies to think about, you can probably be more relaxed about it, but even so, planning ahead will get you better grades in the long run.

And although most teenage students will stay up all night to finish an assignment at some point, if you do this all the time you will get lower grades than you are capable of. Leaving things to the last minute isn't a good habit to get into.

> "Time is very democratic – everyone gets 168 hours a week, whoever they are."

If you plan your studies, you will produce better work, get a better grade at the end of it, have more time to do the other things you want to do, and best of all, you needn't feel guilty about enjoying yourself. Once you have done what you need to do, your time is your own.

Two types of people: two types of time

If all this talk of planning and time management is turning you off, there may be a good reason. People who enjoy planning and are good at it have a different mental image of time from those who live in the here and now and hate planning. If you are one of the latter, keep reading. There really is an explanation for why people have different approaches to planning and time-keeping.

You may have noticed when it comes to getting somewhere on time there are two types of people. Some people come when they are ready, are late more often than not, and often don't really care. They are the people who are involved in everything they do. They live in the present and can be great fun to be with, as they just forget time and enjoy themselves. They are great to have at a party, but it may be annoying if you have to rely on them, since you can never be sure that they will get things done or turn up on time.

The other group of people always plan everything. If they have to go somewhere they arrive early. They hate being late and often look anxious. They tend to worry about what they have done in the past and are always looking ahead to what they have to do next. They would rather organise an event than go to one. They are not very spontaneous and find it hard to let go.

As you read those thumbnail sketches you may have recognised yourself or other people in the descriptions.

Obviously both types of people have their strengths and weaknesses. The first group may be better at relationships, enjoy their social life more, and become more involved with their work. The second group are good at getting things done, but may not enjoy what they are doing so much. They may be rather detached from other people. For instance, thinking about what you've got to do next week when you are with your partner will not make for a very close relationship.

The two types of people are related to the way the brain organises time. Sometimes people who are faced with having to plan their work for the first time say, 'But my brain doesn't work that way,' and they will be right – their brain works in a different way. People who live in the present have a different mental image of time and a different way of talking about it from people who plan.

 ## Living in the present

It is probably more natural to live in the present than to spend our lives planning and checking that we are on target. Our forebears had to live in the present or they could have been prey to a sabre-toothed tiger or woolly mammoth. As small children we live in the present: we want everything now, and forget about what happened a moment ago.

People who live in present time often talk about time as though it were a journey from the past to the future. They talk about someone 'having a great future *ahead* of them'. They tell someone who is dwelling on the past, 'put it *behind* you', or if somebody is going through a difficult time they may say, 'one day you will *look back* on this and laugh'.

People also talk about the 'distant past' or the 'distant future', or 'bringing an event forward' in time. It is as though past and future consists of a straight line with ourselves at 'now', and time arranged chronologically with the past behind us and the future in front of us.

Living in the present

Present
↓

Distant past → Recent past → 👤 → Near future → Distant future

↑
Self

If you are unconsciously organising time in this way, you are living in the present. You probably never think further ahead than a few days or a week.

Planning with calendar time

People who like planning often have a mental image of time as a calendar spread out in front of them reading from left to right. They don't talk about 'putting the past behind them' because both past and future are there for them to see in their mind's eye at any time. They are likely to be conscious of past problems because they keep the memory of them right in front of them. They find it easy to plan ahead because the whole of the future is visible.

Distant past → Recent past → Present → Near future → Distant future

People who live with calendar time talk about time as though it were a commodity. They may say 'time is money', or talk about spending time, or using it, or wasting it. People who talk about 'time being on your side' also live with calendar time.

After reading this, you may already know how you organise time in your brain. If you are not sure, ask yourself, 'Where is the future? Where is the past?' and notice what comes into your mind. Remember that what we are talking about is your *unconscious* image of time – you may not literally see anything.

The benefits of calendar time

To succeed in today's world we need to be able both to work with calendar time and also to live in the present.

When you are in calendar time you can work comfortably with a timetable or diary. This enables you to see how long you've got to do your various tasks. You can look at a week and see whether you are overloaded – if several assignments have to be handed in at once, for instance. You can see when you have to do each task, such as getting hold of books, so that you won't be panicking at the last minute.

You can do better work because you have all the books and materials you need to hand and can give your attention to the work you are doing, knowing that you will be able to finish in time. You have proper thinking time, which is very important at university, because you have to analyse and present arguments and ideas. Regurgitating facts is not enough.

Giving yourself time to think about an assignment and then putting it aside for a few days will make writing it much easier. Imagine your brain is a computer and that you have just given it an instruction to work on your latest assignment. You can then go off and do other things while your unconscious brain goes to work.

By the time you come back to it, you will find the topic seems to be familiar and all sorts of ideas will pop up. This is why you often think of things you could have put in an exam question an hour or so later, and why you think of the perfect riposte just too late.

The good news is that most people can learn to plan when they need to and live in a more relaxed moment-to-moment way for the rest of the time. With experience, most people automatically go from one way of organising time to the other without ever thinking about it. At work they use calendar time and in the evening and at weekends they relax and live in the present. If you want to experiment with your image of time, do the exercise in the box on the next page.

Exercise

Changing your mental image of time

If you want to understand your mental image of time better and be able to change it at will, you need to start by getting a sense of how you imagine time.

Get someone else to ask you, 'Where is the past? Where is the future?', or think about something that happened a few weeks ago, noticing where the thought seems to come from. Then think about something that will happen in a few weeks' time and notice where the thought comes from. Get a sense of a line joining the past, present and future.

When you are aware of this mental timeline you can begin to experiment with it. It may be interesting to do it with someone else who has the opposite timeline from you. But before you start be aware that doing this experiment may feel a little strange to begin with.

To do the experiment, if you are in calendar time, move your timeline so that the past is directly behind you, the future immediately in front of you and the present passes through you. You may feel temporarily disorientated because you cannot see the past or very much of the future. Now put your timeline back again.

If you are in present time, move your timeline in front of you so that past, present and future are in a line a foot or so away from you. This may feel uncomfortable, as though what's happening is detached from you. Now put your timeline back.

Don't feel that you have to go through this process every time you change from one type of time to another. Your brain quickly learns what it has to do and switches easily without your realising it. You will know that you can do it when you feel comfortable with both kinds of timeline.

Working in calendar time

The first thing to do when you get your assignments is to break them down into stages. This is called 'chunking', i.e. breaking something down into small chunks. This makes doing the assignment much more manageable. One of the reasons why people sometimes put off a piece of work is that it sounds too daunting. Once it's broken down you can do a bit at a time. This way you will find you are able to work more efficiently because you can make use of quite small periods of time to do something on your list. You will also have the pleasure of crossing things off!

Think about writing an essay. How many stages are there? Make a list and then compare your answer with the 'Writing an essay' checklist.

Writing an essay

You may be surprised by the number of stages:

- *thinking about what the title means and how you will deal with it*
- *breaking down the subject into sub-topics or headings*
- *getting hold of books and other information*

- *reading and making notes*
- *working out what you want to say under each heading*
- *writing the first draft of your assignment*

- *writing the introduction and conclusion*
- *revising and editing what you have written*
- *checking for spelling and grammar*
- *writing the references, bibliography etc*

Knowing how long to spend on a task

Knowing roughly how long you should spend on each task will help you stay on track and get your assignments in on time without panic. Of course there is no single answer to how long you spend on any task. At first, you may not know how long the various stages will take. If you have no idea, make a point of noticing how much time you are spending – and breaking off for a drink or chat with friends doesn't count as studying!

The commonest mistakes are spending *too much* time on reading and making notes and *too little* time thinking about the topic and revising your work. Before you start reading be clear about what information, ideas, theories etc. you need to cover in your assignment. As you read, remind yourself of what you are looking for. Continuing to collect notes beyond what you need is often a form of procrastination, so when you think you have the key information, move on to the next stage.

Make sure you have left yourself adequate time at the end for revising and editing. People sometimes think that editing is a chore or that it means that you are not good at writing. However, for people who write professionally, it is a key part of the process of getting the words on the paper. All writers, no matter what they are writing, spend time doing this.

As an example, when I was writing this book, I edited on the word processor as I went along, checking that the points I was making were in the right order and that the writing flowed easily and was clear and concise. As I finished the initial draft of each chapter, I read it through and made amendments, sometimes redrafting sections or moving whole paragraphs. When the book was complete, I put it aside for a few days and then read the whole thing through and edited it once more. Then when I had what I thought was the final version, I re-read it and made the final changes before sending it to the publisher.

Be prepared to spend time revising and editing your work and your grades will soar.

Planning backwards

Planning backwards ensures that you know when to start a task to be able to finish on time. For example, if you have to get somewhere on time you start by finding out what train you have to catch. You then add on the time it takes you to get to the station. You now know what time you have to leave. Work out how long it takes you to get ready and you know when you have to start. Anyone who has deadlines to meet will be used to this method of working.

You can apply it to anything you have to do. It may feel strange if you are used to working forwards, not backwards. If so, that is because you have slipped back into present time, instead of calendar time. So put that timetable or calendar in front of you and write on it where the various tasks have to go.

Making a timetable for the term or semester

On page 44 there is a simplified timetable for one term. As an exercise, imagine that you have been given three assignments at the beginning of the term to complete before Christmas. Looking at the checklist on the previous page, write in the tasks so that they are conveniently spaced, or if you don't want to write on the book, do it on a separate sheet.

Remember that some tasks take longer than others. It should be clear when you've done it that you are going to have a more comfortable time if your work isn't all bunched up together.

Of course in real life, timetables are more complicated, but the same principle applies. It is well worth either getting yourself a time planner or drawing one up for yourself. A few minutes spent doing this will save you a lot of anxiety later.

Timetable for one term

	week 1	week 2	week 3	week 4
October	3 assignments rec'd			
November				
December		deadline for 3 assignments		

Making a weekly timetable

When you've made a plan for the term or semester, look at your weekly timetable. It will already have lectures and classes in it and maybe days or slots when you are doing paid work. The rest of the time you can divide up between your studies and the other things you do.

Before you do it, it may be worth keeping a record of how you *actually* spend your time. There are various ways of doing it. If you usually spend an hour or more at one thing, say working in the library, you might note down the amount of time you spend studying, doing paid work, domestic activities, eating and sleeping etc., travelling and leisure. Another method is to jot down what you are doing every half hour during the working day or evening.

Do this for at least one day, or preferably for a week. It may be quite an eye-opener. A group of students in one college I worked at were asked to do this for one week as part of a study skills course. They were amazed at where their time went, and many of them seemed dismayed to think that as students a relatively small percentage of their total time each week was spent studying.

Larks and owls

Before going any further, ask yourself: are you a lark or an owl? Larks are at their best in the morning and are often annoyingly bright at breakfast. Owls wake up at night and hate mornings. Then there is the post-lunch 'dip', when a lot of people feel a bit sleepy and inattentive for an hour or so. Knowing when you are at your brightest is important for planning how to use your time to best advantage. Use the time when you are most alert to do the things that need most thought and do routine things at other times when you are mentally slower.

You are now ready to make yourself the kind of timetable you want, giving yourself reasonable amounts of time to do your various tasks and for leisure activities. Don't fall into the trap of thinking you can only work if you have an hour or more to spare. Make use of short periods of time for returning library books, checking spelling, or even reading one chapter of a book. The time you spend will soon add up.

Exercise

Which of these things would you do when you are most alert? Which of them can you do when you are feeling tired?

- analysing the meaning of the title of an essay

- listing references

- looking for library books

- writing a first draft.

Weekly timetable

	Monday	Tuesday	Wednesday	Thursday	Friday
6–9 a.m.					
9–12 a.m.					
12–3 p.m.					
3–6 p.m.					
6–9 p.m.					
9–12 p.m.					

When to stick to the plan and when not to

The best plan in the world is no good if you don't stick to it. So keep a check on whether you are on target. If you meant to have finished an assignment already but you haven't even started it yet, then you need to think about what's going wrong. Was your plan over-optimistic, or is there some other reason why you have been unable to stick to it? Sometimes people set themselves impossible targets, requiring a huge change in the way they do things. ('I'll get up at five o'clock every morning and work on my latest assignment for three hours before breakfast.')

With the best will in the world, circumstances sometimes overcome us and we get behind. If this is the case, and you don't know why you are slipping, do the diary exercise and see where your time is going. Then see how you can re-organise yourself to get back on track.

And remember that your timetable is meant to be a helpful guide to what you should be doing each day, not a ball and chain. We all need the capacity to be spontaneous sometimes. Sticking too rigidly to a routine can have a deadening effect. Switch things around if you want to, but remember that if you go out instead of doing three hours' work, the three hours will have to be found somewhere else in the week.

Tips for overcoming procrastination

- *admit to yourself that you are procrastinating and what effect it is having*

- *think about how you will feel when it's done*

- *chunk down, so that you don't have to tackle it all at once*

- *commit yourself to doing one small thing*

- *arrange to ring a friend at an agreed time to say you have done the task.*

Procrastination

Procrastination is when you know you should do something but keep putting it off. Every time you put it off, it gets harder to do. You can forget it most of the time and then a horrible feeling creeps over you like a hand gripping your heart. By this time the situation seems to have taken on a life of its own. You begin to have guilt feelings. You know you have to get on with it, yet as time passes, you feel more and more stressed and less able to do it. In the end either circumstances force you to do it, or you make what seems to be a heroic effort to get yourself to do it.

The strange thing is that when you actually do it, it never takes as long to do as you expected, and sometimes, after the initial panic has worn off, you can almost enjoy doing it. At the end of it you feel a great sense of relief, together with a sense of puzzlement that you put it off for so long.

How do I know this? Well, because like most people, now and then I find myself putting some tasks to the bottom of the pile once too often, for no good reason, and realise that I am procrastinating.

Although most people procrastinate occasionally, if it becomes a way of life it eats up time and energy. You create problems for yourself by not doing the task on time. For example, you have to go to your tutor and explain why a piece of work is going to be late. You have to do the work in a rush and feel hassled. You know the grade will be lower when you get it back than it would have been if you'd started on time. It's not a good feeling.

So why do we do it? Sometimes there is some hidden fear around the task. When people procrastinate over academic work, it is often because they are afraid that they might find it difficult. It is one of the facts of life – and learning – that the first time you do a thing is the hardest. From then on, it gets easier.

So the only cure for this kind of procrastination is to tackle the task, knowing that it will become easier as you go along. Chunking down will help. When you can't face setting aside a couple of hours to work on an assignment, you can often do 20 minutes or half an hour, especially if you promise yourself a reward at the end of it. Strangely, you may find that you spend longer working than you intended.

Some people are keen enough to start a task, but procrastinate over finishing it, always finding something else to do before handing it in. If you find yourself reluctant to complete work, you may be a secret perfectionist. You hate to think that someone is going to judge what you have done unless it is perfect. But in life we spend most of our time doing the best we can in the time and with the materials we have been given. Waiting for everything to be right is a way of never doing anything.

There's a saying, 'If a thing's worth doing, it's worth doing well,' meaning that you should take trouble over what you do. However, you sometimes hear people say, 'If a thing's worth doing, it's worth doing *badly*.' What they mean is that if a thing is important then it is worth doing it, even if you can't do it as well as you would like to.

Sometimes leaving things to the last minute is a way of providing ourselves with an excuse. We say, 'I did it at the

---

> **Techniques for overcoming procrastination**
>
> 1. Take it at a running jump. Don't give yourself time to think. Or think about something else as you get started. Once started, you will probably finish.
>
> 2. Get everything out – and then put it away again. Do this for three days and you will be desperate to finish the job.
>
> 3. Shame yourself into doing it by telling everyone – and giving yourself a deadline.

last minute', hoping that people will think that it was very good for a last-minute effort. The unspoken thought is that we could do very well if only we had the time, yet we never dare put ourselves to the test.

The problem with this is that only by doing our best each time do we learn and improve. By copping out, we fail to give ourselves the chance to find out what we are really capable of. But as far as the world is concerned what we have done is the best we can do. The class of degree you get at the end of your course will stay with you for the rest of your life. Far better to work hard and get an upper second than to get a lower second and tell everyone, 'I could have got a first if only ...'

To overcome procrastination, try the techniques below. See what works for you, and apply it in other areas of your life. Ask your friends what works for them and try their techniques as well.

 ## Reference

Sapadin, Linda. (1999) *Beat Procrastination and Make the Grade*. Penguin Books.

money, money, money

Managing money

Managing money is something we have to do all our lives, whether we have a lot of it or a little. The same basic techniques hold good whether you are managing your own personal budget or a multi-million pound budget for a company. Unfortunately, very few people are taught how to manage their own money. Learn this now and you will have a skill that will stand you in good stead for the rest of your life.

Getting in control of your money

Take a sheet of paper and divide it into two columns. Write 'Income' at the top of one column and 'Outgoings' at the top of the other. Start by making a list of *all* your sources of income, using the checklist below. Then write the amounts against each and add it up.

Loan	Earnings – term-time	Savings
Grant		Investment earnings
Authorised overdraft	Earnings – holidays	
	Employer sponsorships	Financial help from family

In the 'Outgoings' column make a list of everything you spend money on – and this means *everything*, including Christmas presents, loo rolls, bars of soap and toothpaste.

The five golden rules for managing money

- know where it is coming from
- know where it is going to
- spend less than you have coming in
- learn where to make economies
- if you have a problem deal with it immediately.

Remember that in term-time you may have to pay for items like laundry, which you probably get for free if you live at home. Use the checklist below to prompt you.

Accommodation	Food
Electricity	Clothes
Gas	Cleaning materials
Phone	Household items (e.g. light bulbs)
Council tax	Laundry
Water charges	TV licence
Insurance	Toiletries
Medical, dentistry, glasses	Mobile
College fees	CDs
Books	Newspapers/ magazines
College materials	Going out
Special equipment	Holidays
Fieldwork expenses	Presents
Computer	Savings/emergency fund
Travel	

Estimate how much you are likely to spend on each item. (If you are not used to doing this exercise, ask parents or other people to help.) Write it down and add it all up. Is the total in the 'income' column the same or (preferably) larger than the total in the 'outgoings' column? If it isn't, you will either have to cut your outgoings or increase your income.

 ## Budgeting

Once you have got your income and outgoings to balance you can make yourself a proper budget. The purpose of this is so that you can check that your outgoings are actually what you have predicted. To help you do this ask your bank for monthly statements and go through them regularly.

Books

Give yourself a budget for the whole term or semester. Divide the sum by the number of courses or subjects you are studying. This is the average amount you have to spend on books for each subject. If you spend more on one subject you will have to spend less on another. Find out how much the books cost on average and work out how many you can afford. Then go through your course information to find out which are the most essential, or ask your tutor. The rest you will have to borrow from the library.

Clothes

Set yourself a budget per month and stick to it.

Day-to-day expenses

This includes travel, food, toiletries, household items, laundry, going out and any impulse buys. Set yourself a weekly budget. Remember that some weeks will be heavier than others, so keep some money in hand for the week when you run out of all those boring household items at once. Get a little notebook and write down *everything* you spend – at least for a few weeks. You may be surprised at where the money is going.

When you go out for the evening, jot down how much money you have on you before you go and write down how much you have left afterwards. That will tell you how much you are spending on a night out. Compare it with your budget. If you overspend one week, cut back the next to get back on track.

"If you find that your outgoings are more than your income you have two choices: either spend less, or earn more."

Phone bills and any household bills

Write down what you expect to spend per month, or per quarter if you pay by the quarter. When your bills come in, check them against your budget. If you have misjudged, look to see where you can economise and adjust your budget accordingly.

Extras

Don't forget all those extra items – holidays, birthday and Christmas presents and the like. Make sure that you have put aside money for them.

Living on less

If you are spending too much, look at the things you have control over, such as calls on your mobile, going out or take-aways. Find a cheaper alternative.

Books

Get as many as you can from the library – which means thinking ahead and getting there before everybody else. Find out if the students' union or any other group has a second-hand book scheme. Ask students who are finishing your course if they have any books they want to get rid of. They may be glad to sell or even give you first-year textbooks they no longer want.

Travel

Get a cheap travelcard, or cycle or walk wherever you can.

Mobiles

Don't use your mobile at peak times. Cut down on phone use and see your friends instead. If you use the phone, be conscious of how long you are on it and don't prolong calls unnecessarily.

Clothes

You don't need fancy gear for going to college. Try charity shops, where you can get incredible bargains, or buy clothes in the sales.

"60% of students experience some degree of difficulty keeping up with bills and credit commitments."

Mori Student Living Report 2003

Food and household goods

Make a list before you go shopping and stick to it. Don't go shopping when you're hungry – you'll buy more than you need.

Buy from a street market if there is one, buy 'own brands' in the supermarket and look for reductions. Use supermarket loyalty cards. You will be glad of the vouchers you get.

Avoid corner shops, which tend to be more expensive. If you are sharing, buy in bulk – it's much cheaper. Forget about take-aways and ready prepared food – get a basic cookbook and learn to cook some simple dishes. Stock up with basic ingredients like dried pasta, tinned tomatoes, cheese and jacket potatoes, which you can always fall back on for a cheap and easy meal.

 ## Household bills

Pay by direct debit and you will get something off your bills. You can also shop around for good deals from different suppliers. In the winter, make sure the central heating is turned off when you are not there. Turn it down when you are in and put on more clothes. Even turning the heating down one degree will make a difference to your bills.

 ## Credit and store cards

Stores love to sign you up with their cards as it makes it so much easier to part you from your money. And unless you settle in full promptly every month you will find in a very short time you have a huge amount of interest to pay back that will make that impulse purchase very expensive indeed. Don't use them.

 ## Holidays

Try a working holiday abroad. You will have a new experience, see a bit of a foreign country and get paid for it.

 ## Concessions

Make sure you know what concessions you are entitled to. Get a student card and use it.

Going out

Use facilities on campus, as these will be cheaper. Look out for any free entertainment that is going. Ration your outings if necessary.

Savings and investments

Put any money you aren't going to spend immediately into an instant-access, high-interest savings account. Make sure that it is low risk and that you have read any small print. Check the weekend newspapers or the Internet for comparative rates.

Saying 'No'

If you tell your friends that you don't have the time or the money to go out, they will usually respect that. But sometimes it is difficult if people keep trying to persuade you. So if you find it difficult to say 'no' to a night out, then take a few moments *now* to think how you will say it.

'No, I can't afford it this week.'

'No, I've got to finish my assignment.'

'No, I'm working tonight.'

'No thanks, but I'd like to go out next week.'

'No thanks, not my kind of thing.'

Make a list of ways of saying 'no' and try them out. Find a few that you feel comfortable saying and that you know you will stick with. Keep it simple. Don't invent excuses or you'll get caught out! Rehearse. Say it with conviction. Remember why you are doing it. Think of not having to worry about money.

And know what you will say when they say: 'Oh come on, just this once.'

'No, not this week, I can't afford it.'

'No, sorry, I'll come out next week when I've finished this assignment.'

'No, some of us have to work for a living.'

'No, I'm not coming out tonight, see you on Saturday.'

'No, I don't want to get into debt, even if you do.'

Give yourself credit for sticking to your guns. Know that you are in control of your own life. If you are in with a crowd that is going out all the time and spending more money than you can afford, start getting to know some people who spend more of their time studying.

Earning while learning

Many students now have to work their way through college. Traditionally, students have taken low-paid work such as stacking supermarket shelves or bar work. There are other alternatives that might be more interesting and pay better. So before you resign yourself to total boredom, start thinking about what you *really* want. Is it:

- an undemanding source of money?

- the most money for the least time?

- convenient travel and working hours?

- general work experience?

- the opportunity to learn something connected with your eventual career?

- a challenge?

Remember that at the end of your course when you are applying for jobs you are likely to be asked at interview what you got out of work as a student. Mumbling, 'I took the first thing that came along. It was very boring and I had to work long hours to make ends meet' won't impress the interviewers with your dynamism. So before you start get clear about what you want from work and how it fits in with your life now and in the future. Write down a list of your priorities.

If you are intending to work during term-time, find out whether your institution has any recommendations about how many hours you should do. (Or, indeed, whether they are happy about you working at all in term-time.) Work out how much you need to earn per week and how many hours you expect to work. Divide the number of hours into the amount you want to earn and you will find out how much you will have to earn per hour. Don't forget that unless your earnings are very low you will have to pay tax and National Insurance.

Do you want to work day-time, evenings or weekends? What effect will your choice have on your studies? Your home life? Your social life? Do you intend to give up your job before exams or do you want a job that will allow you the flexibility to take extra time off around exams?

"52% of undergraduates work to support themselves through their course."

Grad Facts Survey 2002

How far are you prepared to travel? Remember, travelling costs money and is dead time. If the job is one that really meets your criteria it may be worth travelling further for it. If not, you can compare two jobs by subtracting the costs of travel from your earnings and adding the time spent travelling to the number of hours you work. Then work out how much you will get per hour.

Now think about what you have to offer. Think about what skills or knowledge you have. If you have already worked for a while this should be easy. If the work you have done before isn't available part-time or on a temporary basis, think how the skills might be transferred to a different situation. For instance, if your job involved dealing with the public, you may be able to find something else where this experience is an asset. Be creative.

If you haven't worked before, think about what you are learning on your course, such as languages, IT, business or engineering skills. Think about any extra-curricular activities you may have undertaken, e.g. sports coaching or working with young children. List everything that might be useful.

If you are on a non-vocational course and have no previous work experience, consider getting some good IT skills. It's a small investment in time and money that will stand you in good stead in your studies as well as helping you find work.

 ## Finding a job

Many universities now have a job shop. This may be run by the students' union or by the university itself. Check the students' handbook or look at the university website. If you have special skills, see what scope there may be for matching them with the needs of local employers. Find out if there is any seasonal office work. This can be more interesting and better paid than traditional student work. Try a temp agency.

Ask the careers office what information they have about casual work. Ask if the university employs students for casual work, in the library for example. If you have some idea of what you would like to do, phone up employers and ask if they have anything suitable. Ask, ask, ask. Look in the

Don'ts

- Don't get involved with anything dodgy – it's not worth it
- Don't get stuck in a boring low-paid job – look for something better
- Don't take a 'commission only' job – chances are you will earn peanuts
- Don't take something that sounds too good to be true – it probably is
- Don't get stuck with a job you hate – you have choices.

local paper. If you want a job in a shop, cafe or supermarket, look in their windows.

If you've got money problems

If the sums just don't add up and you think you may have special circumstances, go and see the student welfare officer or financial adviser. Many institutions have hardship funds that you can apply for, and there are charities that can help. There may also be benefits you can apply for. Do this *now*, as you may find that the applications take a little while to be considered.

If you know that you are overspending, *stop*. At this moment you have two alternatives: you *could* get into serious debt, or you can take action *now* and pull your finances back under control. If you run up an unauthorised overdraft you will pay sky-high interest charges, and to add insult to injury the bank will charge you a considerable sum for every letter that they write to you about it. So if you've got a problem, talk to the bank *before* they send you a letter.

If you get a letter from the bank, make an appointment to see them. In the meantime work out where the money is going. Write down all your spending – and that means everything. You may be surprised. Do your budget again. Work out how much you can pay back per month before your appointment. You will usually find that you can come to an arrangement with them. Stick to it.

If too much money is going on credit cards, cut them up before you read any further. If you are spending too much time on your mobile, leave it behind unless you *really* need it. Put it somewhere where you can't easily get to it. Decide on what you will do instead – it could be something simple like going for a short walk or listening to some music for 10 minutes. Every time you think of using it, repeat the new activity.

"When you are in a hole, stop digging"

If you are spending too much time on going out, set a limit, give yourself a budget and stick to it. When you go out, only take with you what you are prepared to spend. On the days you would have gone out, create an alternative. Take on more paid work, for example. This will help to clear your overspend and as a bonus you won't be able to spend money while you are working. Or go to the library and spend more time studying and improving your grades. Or find some free leisure activities.

Be clear in your own mind why you are doing all this. Then tell the people who will support you. Say it with conviction. Ask them to check with you to see that you have done what you said you would. Knowing someone is going to ask you tends to stiffen your resolve! Think about what keeps you going – do you want someone to praise you? Tell them. Or do you like a bit of competition? If so, find someone in the same position and set yourselves targets and compare notes on a regular basis.

Don't tell people who put you down. Keep away from them, and when you see them, keep your own counsel. You don't need them.

Take a day at a time. Can you give up just this once? Yes, you can. Think about what is enjoyable about the new situation. Keep doing it until you have got a new habit. Monitor your money situation and watch it improving, week by week and month by month. You may find that you like the feeling of being in control.

Points to ponder

- What have I learnt from this?
- What have I learnt about myself?
- What have I learnt about others?
- How can I apply this learning?

If you've got SERIOUS debts

Keep reading. There IS an answer.

If you owe a lot of money the problem has probably been going on for a while and you know that you should do something about it. Maybe you've tried to push the thoughts away. Maybe you've pretended it wasn't happening. Or maybe you've talked about it endlessly but haven't done anything about it. Maybe you've been using drink or drugs to deaden the anxiety.

But you know, really, that the only person who can change this situation is you. Think ahead to next year: will you be under an even larger pile of debts, or will you be thinking how glad you are that you took action now?

How would you feel if you knew that one phone call or visit would lift the burden? It just might. Perhaps you feel 'stuck'? Do you remember when you were little and had a plaster on your leg and you tried to pull it off agonisingly slowly? Then someone told you to rip if off quickly. And when you did, by the time the pain had reached your brain the plaster was off and it was done with. So act straight away, before you have time to think about it.

"The longest journey starts with a single step"

If your university has a drop-in centre for students with financial problems, go along now. (Look at Chapter 10 for information about student support services if you don't know what's likely to be available.) If you need to phone for an appointment, do it quickly. If you feel flooded by anxiety as you do it, that's OK. The feelings will subside as soon as you have done it. What's more, you will be on the road to success in solving the problem.

Now you can relax. Reward yourself. Maybe you want to tell someone. (If you phone them, ask them to phone you back!) Or you may need to do something physical to get rid of the feelings of stress in your body. Go for a run or a swim.

If you made an appointment, keep it. Be prepared to get help from more than one person if need be, now that you have started down this route. The first step is the hardest, so now that you have taken that first step, keep going.

Reducing anxiety

If you feel very anxious every time you think about dealing with the problem, here are some tried and tested ways of getting on top of it. Try the following techniques and find out what works best for you.

Techniques

Points to ponder:

- *What have you learnt from this experience?*

- *How has your attitude to money changed?*

- *How has your attitude to yourself changed?*

- *What have you gained from this experience?*

- *What will you do differently in future?*

- Make a list of the things you have to do. Then do one thing each day, early in the morning. Once you have done it, stop thinking about the problem and enjoy your day.

- Notice what thoughts are going through your head. If they aren't positive, change them to ones that are. How would it be if there was a voice inside your head saying: 'Go on, you can do it'? Every time you find yourself saying something negative inside your head, *stop* and say something positive instead. See how many times you can do this a day.

- Imagine how you are going to feel when it is all over. Where will you be? What will you be doing? Who will you be with? What do you see? What do you hear? What are you feeling?

Whatever techniques you use, track your successes. Keep a notebook and write down how many times you do these exercises and which ones work best for you. Note how many times you have done them successfully. Note every step you take to bring your finances under control. You will soon have a long list. When you need to remind yourself that you are succeeding, look at the list. Imagine it growing as the debts shrink.

"Change your thoughts and you change the world."

Norman Vincent Peale

You can do it. And by doing it you will have learnt a lot about yourself and how you can manage your own life.

 ## Further reading

Balancing Your Books: the ECCTIS/CRAC guide to student finance. CRAC and ECCTIS.

Hopkins, I and K. (1997) *Budgeting for Students: how to get the most out of your time at college on limited financial resources.* How To Books.

Thomas, G. (2003) *Students' Money Matters: a guide to sources of finance and money management.* Trotman.

chapter 6

other people are different

At university you will probably come into contact with a wider range of people than you have before. They may have different social, religious or ethnic backgrounds, different values, expectations or lifestyles. You will meet people not only at university itself but on holiday or term-time jobs and on work placements. Whether you are a school leaver or a mature student, you can expect to meet people who are different from you and different from the people you have known before. This can be a very rewarding part of university life.

You will also meet people with different ways of seeing the world and dealing with it. While you are studying on your own, this may not seem too important. However, when you have to do a group project or work with or for other people, the different ways in which people approach a task can be confusing or lead to arguments. It may seem that others are being just plain difficult in the way that they approach tasks.

"All the world's a little odd, save thee and me – and even thee's a little odd."

Proverb

Ways in which people differ

Psychologists have devised many different ways to classify people. The supporters of each system would probably claim that theirs is the most useful way of thinking about how people differ. For everyday purposes it probably doesn't matter too much *how* you think about it, as long as you *do* think about it. Being aware that someone else has a different way of approaching life is the first step to understanding what they feel comfortable with and accommodating it so that you both get what you want.

We have already looked at some differences between people. In Chapter 2 we looked at different ways people motivate themselves. In Chapter 4 we looked at how different ways of thinking about time were linked to two different personality types. We are now going to look at some other ways in which people are different.

 ## Carrots or sticks?

In Chapter 2 we said that some people motivated themselves by imagining the worst thing that could happen if they didn't act, whereas other people prefer to think of achieving their goal. You can think of this as carrots and sticks: do you need a reward for doing something, or do you need a stick to be beaten with if you don't?

Although most people probably respond better to rewards than punishments, the habit of thinking mainly about your end goals or mainly about the problems you may encounter is one of the ways in which people differ. If you prefer a carrot to a stick, you are the kind of person who is good at setting goals and who knows what they want. You have energy and enthusiasm. You don't get put off easily, but you may not see the problems that can arise out of a plan.

If you respond better to the stick, you will enjoy having problems to solve. You will be motivated by deadlines, and you will be good at troubleshooting. You will be likely to spot the problems in any plan. On the other hand you may have difficulty focusing on your goal and may keep fixing whatever problems come your way.

Confusing conversations no. 1:

'Have you really thought this through? There could be a lot of problems to overcome.'

'You're so cynical. Whenever I tell you what I want to do, all you do is tell me about the problems.'

Ideally we need to be able to work with carrots *and* sticks. Some people can do this, but the majority seem to prefer one or the other. In a team, of course, it is possible to have people with different approaches. The person who likes 'carrots' can devise plans and keep the team on track, and one who likes 'sticks' can identify the problems that arise and solve them. This works well when people respect each others' capabilities.

 ## Starter or finisher?

If you find that starting something new is exciting and motivating, you probably like doing projects because you can choose your own thing. You may find it hard to decide what to focus on, because you love having choices. Once the choices have been narrowed down, the project may seem less appealing to you. Routine tasks such as editing and correcting your work will quickly bore you. Your challenge is to put as much energy into completing work as starting it.

However if you are a finisher you will want to know how to do something before you start. You like to know the right way of doing things, so projects which you are free to tackle in your own way make you feel uncomfortable. You are good at editing your work and checking it thoroughly for mistakes. Your challenge is to be prepared to trust your own ideas and follow them.

Confusing conversations no. 2:

'Let's do this the way we did the last group exercise. It worked really well.'

'Hey, that's boring. Let's try a different way.'

With academic work, the emphasis on starting and finishing will be different depending on the subject and the way it is taught. Generally speaking, arts subjects and the creative arts in particular may be better for starters, and science or engineering may be better for finishers. However, academic work requires some of each – the creativity and enthusiasm of the starter and the accuracy of the finisher.

 ### *Big picture or detail?*

If you like the big picture, you like overviews, summaries and ideas. You take ideas in the order that they come to you, rather than in sequence. You don't like getting bogged down in detail. You get irritated by it and like to get to the point.

If you like detail, you will want to do everything in the right order, concentrating only on what comes before or after. You are as specific as possible about whatever you are doing, and if you are interrupted, you will probably begin again.

Confusing conversations no. 3:

'How did you get on with your new date?'

'Well, we met up at nine p.m., but his car wouldn't start, so we ...'

'Yeah, but did you like him? Are you going to see him again?'

'I'm telling you. We met up at nine p.m., but his car wouldn't start ...'

If you know you clearly fall into one or other of these categories you will probably be able to call to mind conversations with people who were the opposite. If you like the big picture you will have had conversations with people who 'can't see the wood for the trees'. If you go with the detail, you may have met some rude people who switch off or interrupt you when you are trying to explain something. Now you know why.

 ## Tasks or people?

Do you focus on the task or the people involved? If you focus on the task, you will want to get it done, and that will be more important to you than the feelings of the people involved. This doesn't mean that you ignore people's feelings – it's just that you see them as only a part of what is going on. If you focus on people, you will be mainly concerned with how people feel or react to what is happening. The task is secondary.

Confusing conversations no. 4:

'Don't you realise people are feeling really upset about this project?'

'Yes, but we've got to do it anyway and if we spend all our time examining our feelings we'll never get it finished and we'll all end up with bad marks.'

Being aware of this is important if you have to work in a group. The task-centred person will get frustrated by the way that the people-centred person keeps bringing things back to how people are feeling, because they are worried that the task won't get done in time. The people-centred person will feel that what is most important is being ignored.

Other people's judgement or your own?

Do you look to other people to know how well you have done or do you decide for yourself? Do you seek other people's opinions or do you make up your own mind? If someone tells you something, do you accept it or do you go and check it out for yourself? Do you need lots of feedback or do you tend to ignore it?

Of course in some situations it may be better to rely on feedback from others, for instance your tutors' comments on assignments, or any situation where you are starting something new, or have to follow instructions. In other situations, you may need to rely on your own judgement.

It may sound as though people who always rely on their own judgement are very confident. Sometimes they are.

Confusing conversations no. 5:

*'Everybody's saying they like that new
bar that's opened, so it must be good.
Let's go.'*

*'Why should I like it just because
everybody else does?'*

However, some people rely on their own judgement in a negative way. For instance, they may make negative judgements about themselves and refuse to listen to people who tell them anything to the contrary. ('I know I'm rubbish at it and I don't care what you think.') They will stick to their own view, no matter what anybody else says.

 ### Working alone or with others?

Some people really like to work alone. If this is you, you like to take sole responsibility for what you are doing and hate being interrupted when you are working. If you are working on your own project you will be quite happy to do it without talking about it to anyone else. You have good concentration and can ignore what is going on around you. You hate group projects. If group projects are part of your course, remember that for a little while at least co-operation is the name of the game.

If you prefer to work with others, you will love the opportunities for discussion and group activities. You may feel stuck and unmotivated when you have to work entirely on your own.

Fortunately, most people are comfortable with working on their own part of the time and part of the time co-operating with others. But if you come across someone who is very hostile to group work, remember that they are not being difficult on purpose. They may respond better if they have a clear-cut role within the group.

First person, second person, third person

So far we have looked at some examples of how people differ in the way they set about their work. But there are other ways of classifying people's approaches to life. For instance, when something happens, do you immediately think of what effect it will have on you, do you put yourself in the shoes of the other person concerned, or do you stand outside it all, looking on dispassionately?

You can probably think of people who always react by thinking about themselves. If someone has an car accident, their first thought is, 'Damn, now I won't get a lift.' At work, if someone gets the sack, they think, 'How does it affect my job?' If a flatmate does something annoying such as leaving the milk out of the fridge until it goes off, they think, 'They're so selfish. Now I can't have milk in my coffee.'

Whatever they do and whatever happens they think of themselves first. In conversation they say 'I' a lot. They never stop to think that there might be another point of view. I call this way of looking at the world 'first person', because these people always put themselves first.

Another group of people always put other people first and themselves second. If someone has a car accident, their first thoughts are about the other person – whether they are all right and the problems they might have until their car is repaired.

If someone says to them, 'How will you manage without a lift?', they say, 'Oh, it doesn't matter about me, I'll cope.' If someone gets the sack, they will rush to commiserate. They feel guilty because they haven't been fired too. And if a flatmate is always leaving the milk out and it goes off, they take on the job of making sure that it's put away. And if it goes off, they buy fresh milk themselves and make excuses for their flatmate.

Confusing conversation no. 6:

First person: 'Emma's ducked out of the team. Apparently her mother's ill. It's really annoying – now I've got to find someone else at the last minute.'

Second person: 'Is her mother very ill? Emma must be upset. Anyway, I'm sure you'll find someone.'

Third person: 'This happened last time. Would it make more sense to have a reserve? Then we could cope if someone had to drop out.'

Then there are the observers. They are the third person watching what's going on between the other two, but not getting involved. They notice dispassionately and can often explain situations. If someone has a car accident they will say, 'I told him weeks ago he should have had that car serviced.' If someone has been fired they say, 'If you'd studied the trends you could see that department was vulnerable.' They watch the saga of the milk and say, 'You always let her get away with it. She'll never take any responsibility around the flat if you always do it for her.'

First person role

Being the first person in your life is good if you are in a competitive situation. It gives you an edge and you aren't slowed down by worrying about someone else or why something happened. If you work in a company, it will be a good thing to think instantly: how does this affect us?

But even in a competitive or organisational setting it can be good to be second person sometimes. Understanding how your competitors are positioning themselves in the market and what your customers want can help your own company to develop a unique selling point that will attract more business.

Police officers and military leaders have to be able to put themselves into the position of the criminal or the enemy to understand what they are most likely to do. If you play a competitive sport, getting under the skin of your opponent will help you understand their strengths and weaknesses and enable you to play the best game you can against them.

And it can be good in any situation to step back from time to time, to plan and take the longer view.

Of course if you are always first person in your personal and social life, always seeing things only from your own point of view and never reflecting or seeing things from the other person's point of view, you will quickly get labelled selfish. People who are always saying 'me, me, me' are pretty boring people to be with. They tend to make more mistakes than other people because they never learn from other people's experience. So put yourself in the 'second person' position sometimes.

Second person role

Being able to empathise with others will always help you to make friends. People like to be listened to and to have someone to share their problems and successes with. Being second person is appropriate for some professions, such as acting, or the caring professions, in which clients are looking for support.

However, getting sucked too deeply into a client's problems may mean that you lack the objectivity to help them. If you are performing, you need to be able to stand back and assess your own performance, and you need to have the push and competitive edge to succeed.

In more competitive situations, spending too much time in second person will result in your being left behind. If this is the position in which you feel most comfortable, you will probably hate anything competitive anyway.

If you are always second person, you can become a doormat, never living your own life. People around you will

Exercise

Think of something that has happened to you recently where someone else has been involved. Or think of someone that you wish you could get on with better. Think of a specific occasion with this person, when things didn't go as well as you would like.

Think first of all how it feels from your own point of view. What are you feeling as you bring it to mind? What are you thinking?

Next imagine yourself in the other person's shoes. How do you imagine they might be feeling? What might they be thinking? How might they see you?

Now get some distance from it. Imagine you are a fly on the wall as you look at yourself and the other person. What would make the situation better? What do you need to do to change it?

Now experience it from your own point of view again, taking with you all the knowledge you've gained from the exercise.

How is it different?

fall into the habit of expecting you to be the one to sort out their problems. They will act as if everything is your responsibility and you are at fault if anything goes wrong.

Another way of living as second person is to live through your children. If you have been on the receiving end of this or know someone who has, you will be aware of how unfair this is to the children. We all need to be ourselves and to fulfil our own hopes and dreams, not somebody else's.

Third person role

Someone who is always the third person observing the other two will often know more about what's going on. They will often like research, using data, doing experiments or building things. They like to know why things work the way they do. Third person can be a great place to be when you need to plan and make decisions, because you are able to weigh up all the pros and cons dispassionately.

However, if you are always in third person, you can end up never being involved with your own life. If all your decisions are made logically and never through passion, your existence may seem colourless. You may lose touch with your own feelings and hence with other people's.

This is not helpful in a relationship. There is nothing more annoying than someone dispassionately analysing your behaviour when you get angry with them. And, although you may be very good at solving problems for people, sometimes what they want is someone who knows how they feel and can sympathise. Getting this wrong can lead to lots of problems in relationships.

Tutors as first, second and third person

Tutors as much as anybody else may have a preference for one of these roles. The tutor in first person may be a great performer because they like to be centre stage. You may enjoy their lectures because they are so lively. Alternatively, they may see their main route to promotion lying in research, in which case you may feel you are taking second place some of the time.

Tutors in second person are always ready to listen to your problems. They may be personal tutors, or they may have no formal role but be the one everyone goes to for help and advice because they are so sympathetic.

Tutors in third person will be good at giving you a balanced picture of their subject. They may make it less interesting than a tutor in first person, but they will be thorough. If you ask for advice they will give it to you, but they won't take a personal interest in you.

 ## First, second and third person in academic work

Traditionally academic work has been done in the third person. You are asked to be objective, carry out experiments, or weigh up the evidence for and against a certain theory or explanation. You write assignments as though you are standing back observing what happened.

If you studied history in the past you would probably write in your essays something like, 'The war was caused by economic change' or whatever the reason might be. You wouldn't be expected to take sides and say who was in the right, but to observe and analyse what went on.

If you have done history at school recently you will probably have done exercises in which you had to imagine what it was like to be, say, a child during the bombing and you will have written your account as though you were that child experiencing it. You may have written in your essay, 'I was very frightened', for example.

In some subjects, such as literature, you might be expected to give your own personal response to a poem you have read and to say how you felt. There again, you might be expected to analyse how the poem produced that effect on you.

Although some subjects lend themselves more to one approach than the other – science is normally written in the third person, for example – it often depends on the way a subject is taught. Tutors teaching the same subject may have different views about what they want from you. To get it straight, ask if they want you to stick to the evidence or if they want you to express your own views. Do they want you to bring in your own experience or that of other people? How much of this is appropriate?

This may occasion some debate, but it should help clarify for everybody what the tutor is looking for and why different tutors want different approaches.

Team spirit

Nowadays it is common for students to have to work together for part of the time, sometimes on an assessed project. This is good training for you if you have had little work experience, since most jobs require some element of teamwork. It is a good learning experience to be able to work constructively with others, to know what your own best contribution is likely to be, and to be able to appreciate other people's strengths.

At work, managers will try to put together a balanced team so that all the personal skills that are needed will be available to the team as a whole. So you might get a team with a starter who will be an ideas person and an enthusiast, an observer who can be critical and spot the problems, a problem solver and a finisher so that the job gets done. It may also be useful to have someone who is good at second person so that personal problems within the team can be addressed.

At university it is unlikely that you will be in a group that is made up in this way. You may be allowed to choose your own group, in which case you will probably choose people you already get on with. On other occasions you may be put in a group randomly. You may then find that your group is not well-balanced. Imagine what it would be like if everyone were permanently in first person! You may also find that the group lacks certain personal skills.

Thinking about the different skills that people can bring is a good way of learning to value other people's contribution and learning about your own strengths and weaknesses.

Exercise

If you could choose a well-balanced team out of the people you know, who would you choose and why? What role would you yourself play in the team?

 Further reading

Quilliam, S. (2003) *What Makes People Tick? The ultimate guide to personality types*. Element.

chapter 7

the future starts now

If you are in your first year, or are preparing to go to university, your thoughts are probably on your studies rather than what you will do after you leave. Surely you don't have to think about a career until your third year?

Wrong. For two main reasons – you may make the wrong choices for the career you eventually want to take up, and you need to build a CV throughout your time at university.

The academic choices you make now may cut down your career options, or at best may mean that you have to do an extra year, which is time-consuming and expensive.

If you have any thought of going into a profession, such as law, teaching or psychology, check out the requirements as soon as possible. You may need a particular subject for entry into the profession that you don't need to get into university. For example, teachers need maths. You may also find that combined degrees may not allow you entry to some professions, such as law, without doing further study. If possible find out *before* you get to university.

If you are on a vocational course, check out the different specialisms and what they entail before deciding on your second-year options. Your university careers service will run employer workshops where you will be able to find out what is involved and what you will need to do to get the best chance of a job. Keep an open mind and don't dismiss possibilities out of hand.

If you are doing a traditional single-subject honours or a modular degree, you can to some extent keep your options open until later, since in most cases employers will be looking for people with trained minds and skills rather than subject specialisms.

"Unless you know for sure exactly what you want to do, keep your options open. All too often third-year students find that they have made the wrong choices. This can bring a lot of heartache or needless expense."

Sally Elks, Careers Service Manager, London Metropolitan University

Nevertheless, beginning to explore the range of possibilities sooner rather than later may give you some ideas about what kind of career you might be interested in. Start to think about what appeals to you and why. Base your views on *facts*, not some vague ideas you may have of what it is all about. Look through leaflets on different careers, go to talks arranged by your careers service, take opportunities for work shadowing, talk to anybody you know. Find out what qualifications you would need to get into any of the careers that sound interesting.

Why you need to start work on your CV now

It is vital that you build up a good CV as you go along. Nowadays a CV is not just a list of qualifications gained and jobs done. Employers will want to see what skills you have gained along the way and you will need to make sure that what you do in your academic work, paid work and other activities provides you with the skills employers are looking for. This is not something you can do at the last minute.

And when you eventually come to apply for jobs, you will find that application forms have some very tough questions on them. A typical question might be: 'Describe a situation that illustrates your ability to resolve problems. Tell us what the problem was, your strategy for resolving it and the outcome.'

If you haven't thought about it until you actually start applying it will be very difficult to answer the question. But if you think about this type of question as you go along you will be able to produce much better answers when the time comes.

What employers are looking for

Employers have very carefully thought out requirements when they are recruiting. For instance, if they are looking for particular vocational knowledge and skills they will be targeting specific courses at specific universities that they know turn out graduates who have what they are looking for.

Some employers don't require specific skills and knowledge, but are looking for, say, a scientific background or a good grasp of statistics or a relevant degree. Some will be looking to recruit from a certain type of university. Blue chip companies, for instance, recruit mainly from Oxbridge and the older universities.

Other companies, including those that have started recruiting graduates more recently, may be looking to the newer universities to provide them with trainable graduates who have personal skills they can build on.

> "We believe that to be successful at Marks and Spencer graduates need to have developed their life skills as well as obtaining a degree. Life skills would include team working, good communication and leadership skills."

John McElwee, Graduate and BPP Campaign Manager, Marks and Spencer

Skills and attributes

So what are these skills that employers are looking for? They are the kind of skills and attributes that make you a better employee – someone who fits in with the company and who is successful. Sometimes these are called *transferable* skills, because they can be transferred from one situation to another. IT skills are a good example because you can use them in a variety of different situations.

Many of the skills that employers are looking for are to do with communicating and working well with others. Of these, teamwork has been rated by many employers as their number one priority. Other skills, such as problem solving, may be more intellectual, and some are more to do with your personality, such as being persistent and not giving up easily when faced with a problem. If you look at any advertisements for graduates you will see that they list the skills and attributes they are looking for. In some cases these may be as important as the class of degree.

You can't manufacture these skills in the last few months at university, so you will need to think about how you are

Skills and attributes that employers are looking for:

Technical skills and knowledge	Personal skills	Attributes
research	teamwork	self-belief
analysis	leadership	self-confidence
problem solving	communication skills	self-motivation
numeracy	motivating people	go-getting
IT	relating to others	persistence
evaluating results	managing people	ability to work under pressure
report writing	negotiating skills	initiative
presentations	prioritising	adaptability
business awareness	planning	ability to respond to change
customer awareness	organising events	creativity
	seeing things through	
	assertiveness	
	ability to go on learning	

going to develop them. Many courses now include oral presentations, group projects and problem-solving activities. If you want to acquire skills through your academic work, look at how courses are taught. Also check to see if work placements are available, as this is another way to develop your skills and will look on your CV.

Other opportunities may come from paid work. Look for jobs that offer you some potential for development, for instance dealing with the public, or anything where you have to use your initiative, do something different, or take on more responsibility. Remember that other people will be doing this and that you will eventually be competing with them for jobs.

> "40% of all graduate employment opportunities are open to graduates of any discipline."

If you don't have to do paid work during term-time, consider volunteering or tutoring school students. Undertake some sports coaching, or get involved with student societies and clubs – become an active member of the students' union, organise events, or be a student representative.

If you are a mature student, you will probably already have many of the kinds of skills employers are looking for. Think about the skills you have, and those you need to develop. Look for ways in which you can do this.

You will also probably have many of the attributes that employers will be looking for. For instance, you can claim to be good at decision making – deciding to go back to university after working or bringing up children (or both) is not a decision you will have taken lightly. You probably have to juggle your priorities to manage your studies and the rest of your life. And it is likely that you have a high degree of persistence to keep going. Start thinking about yourself in this light and make a list of what you already have to offer.

 ### Evidence of skills

You will eventually need some kind of evidence that you have acquired the skills or have the attributes you say you have. If you are assessed on any of them, this will be straightforward, as you will be able to tell the prospective employer what grade you achieved. When you are choosing options, check this out as it will make life easier later on.

If skills aren't assessed as part of your coursework, you will need to think hard about what you can offer as evidence. In this case you will need to think of what you have done that

Exercise

Use the questions below to guide you on how to record what you've done:

What precisely is the event you are recording? (e.g. Group Psychology project at end of Year 1.)

What did you do? ('Kept the group on schedule and to time.')

How did you do it? ('Reminded the group of what we had to achieve and the time we had to do it in.')

What happened? ('The group listened to me and began to become more task-focused and time-conscious.')

What was the result? ('It wasn't formally assessed but we were commended for our results.')

What are the skills you demonstrated? ('Ability to lead others, to get the task done successfully, and to get it done on time')

will demonstrate your skills. This will be much easier if you work on it as you go along.

If you are working on team skills, for example, reflect on how you are performing in the group. What do you bring to it? When have you made an important contribution? What is your role in the group? Look back at Chapter 6 for some ideas to get you started.

It will be much easier to do this if you keep a file and start writing down all the examples you think of. It will show you what you are good at, where the gaps are, and will help you to create a plan to build up your CV. Eventually, you can draw on the file when you start applying for jobs. You will then find that you have done most of the hard work already!

The example on page 86 is taken from academic work. You will need to go through the other areas of your life (paid work, volunteering etc.) to make a complete record. And don't forget, if you have been bringing up children, you will have developed lots of skills, such as meeting deadlines (e.g. getting children to school on time) and negotiating, (getting them to tidy their rooms). No doubt you will be able to think of lots more examples.

Building a winning CV

Traditional CVs list your qualifications and work or other experience in chronological order – see the example on page 88. Application forms usually follow the same format. To get work as a student this is probably the kind of thing you will have to produce. Make sure that you highlight your achievements and anything unusual that you have done that might be of interest to an employer. Your careers service will probably run a CV checking service to help you do this.

But to build up a CV as a graduate, you will need to draw on the log of skills that you have been compiling and make

Traditional CV format

Name	Lucy Brown
Address	9 Barrow Road
	Meyton, SL3 9DE
Tel:	020 856 4123
Date of birth	1981
Nationality	British

Education

2003	B.A. 2.1 Combined Studies, English and History of Art – Meyton University
2000	A levels – 3
1998	GCSEs – 9, including maths

Work experience

2003	Work shadowing local MP for 2 weeks
2002	Receptionist at Hoebury Manufactures plc (summer job 2 months)
2002	Library assistant, part-time – Meyton University (term-time)
2001	Receptionist at Hoebury Manufactures plc (summer job 2 months)
2001	Bar assistant, part-time, Cow and Gate Pub, Meyton (term-time)

Interests

Walking, drama, cinema.

Further information

Most of my work experience has involved dealing with people. I had to work under pressure as a bar assistant in a very busy pub and coped successfully with the public in all its moods. I have taken part in an annual pantomime in my home town for the past five years and this has given me confidence in presenting myself.

I learnt a great deal about people's problems and how they are dealt with from shadowing my local MP.

I am computer literate and can wordprocess and use databases.

Referees

S. Muhika (tutor)
Meyton University
Meyton
SL3 7BE

J. Green (Director, HR)
Hoebury Manufactures plc
23 Moss Way
Hoebury, BE2 6ED

Skills-based CV format

Name	Lucy Brown
Address	9 Barrow Road
	Meyton, SL3 9DE
Tel:	020 856 4123
Date of birth	1981
Nationality	British

Communication skills

Presented a report to fellow students and director of local art gallery as part of my third-year project. Keen contributor to the group discussions that form a regular part of my course.

Teamwork

We had regular group work as part of my course and had to produce work as a team effort. I played the lead part in a local pantomime last year and have taken part in it for the previous four years. This has taught me a lot about the need for people to pull together to succeed.

Customer awareness

Working in the bar of the Cow and Gate, as a library assistant and as a receptionist at Hoebury Manufactures plc has given me varied experience of dealing with customers and staff at all levels.

Numeracy and IT

I have GCSE maths and can wordprocess and use spreadsheets.

Education

2003	B.A. 2.1 Combined Studies, English and History of Art – Meyton University
1999	A levels – 3
1997	GCSEs – 9, including maths

Work experience

2003	Work shadowing local MP for 2 weeks
2002	Receptionist at Hoebury Manufactures plc (summer job 2 months)
2002	Library assistant, part-time – Meyton University (term-time)
2001	Receptionist at Hoebury Manufactures plc (summer job 2 months)
2001	Bar assistant, part-time, Cow and Gate Pub, Meyton (term-time)

Referees

S. Muhika (tutor)	J. Green (Director, HR)
Meyton University	Hoebury Manufactures plc
Meyton	23 Moss Way
SL3 7BE	Hoebury, BE2 6ED

them a major factor. So as well as keeping a list of your educational qualifications and work and other experience, it will be really useful to develop a *skills-based* CV. This means that the main information about what you have to offer is listed under the skills you have. (See the example on page 89.)

By building up a CV in this way you can begin to see what skills you have and where the gaps are. It will also help you to match your skills against any careers that you are interested in.

Your skills-based CV should use a few key headings. Employers most frequently ask for communication skills, including report writing and presentations, and interpersonal skills, such as teamwork, managing others, and leadership, so make sure those are on your list. Group other skills together.

Look at what you have left out. If you haven't put numeracy, for example, you need to think about how this will affect your career choice. There are lots of jobs nowadays in which you have to manage a budget or be able to understand statistics. If you know you have gaps, find out what you can do to fill them.

There are loads of books and many useful websites on preparing CVs. You will find some of them listed at the end of this chapter. Your careers service will probably stock some of the books or you will find them in the library.

Getting to know yourself

Analysing your skills is one part of getting to know yourself, finding out what you are good at or enjoy doing, and what you have to offer employers. But to determine what kind of job you might want to do, you will need to be much more self-aware – of your interests, your values and your personality. This is a continuous activity that will guide your choices throughout university and will ultimately help you to choose the right career.

Start by writing down a list of your interests. As well as leisure activities, think about what you like reading about or what kind of television programmes you enjoy. Think about the times when you've felt most fulfilled, and the dreams you had when you were a kid. What does this tell you? Think also about the people you most admire and the things they've done, and about what *you* would most like to achieve. You will begin to build up a list of things you want to find out more about.

Values are the things that really matter to you in your future career. Knowing what is important to you will help to steer you towards some kinds of careers and away from others. Look at the list of values below to give you an idea. Then write your own top ten. Put them in order of priority. Repeat this exercise from time to time: your values may change.

Values

independence	being part of a team	variety
working with people	opportunities for promotion	status
helping others	challenge	pressure
security	good working relationships	excitement
competition	creativity	getting results

Now think about your personality. In Chapter 6 we looked at some of the ways in which people differ. By thinking about other people, you will already have come to some conclusions about yourself. Are you a starter or a finisher? Are you a team player or do you like to work alone? Do you go for the big picture or do you like to work with detail?

Do you like to create something new, or do you like to stick to a known procedure? Are you task-focused or people-focused? Are you a competitive go-getting type, do you want to help others or are you most comfortable in a situation where you can stand back and analyse?

By getting a sense of who you are and what you want, you will find making choices about your second- and third-year options will become much easier.

Your careers service

Get to know your careers service in your first year. They may be able to help you to get jobs by listing vacancies and helping with CVs. They may have an e-mail service that will alert you to anything that is of interest to you. Find out.

Does your careers service offer

- career management courses

- careers fairs

- careers guidance interviews

- computer-aided guidance programmes

- employer presentations

- help with CVs

- drop-in service

- information library on careers and employers

- job opportunities

- mentoring

- on-line CVs

- psychometric testing

- student development activities to help you develop skills and build up your CV

- student tutoring opportunities

- vacancy listings

- volunteering opportunities

- workshops.

Career management courses

Some universities now run career management courses. They will take you through all the things you need to help you find out more about yourself – your strengths, your interests, your personality; careers that will suit you, and how to make effective applications.

Look out for them. If they are offered on a voluntary basis, take advantage of them. They will make your life so much easier in the long run. They may be on-line or a regular course. They may be compulsory or optional, assessed or non-assessed. They usually take place in your second year. Ask your careers service what is available.

 ## Further reading

Corfield, R. (2003) *Preparing your own CV: how to improve your chances of getting the job you want*. 3rd ed. Kogan Page.

Higginbottom, G. (2002) *CVs for Graduates: CV writing skills to make the most of your student experience*. 2nd ed. How To Books.

Houston, K. (2002) *Winning CVs for First-time Job Hunters*. Trotman.

Jones, A. (2000) *How to Write a Winning CV: the best guide for the perfect CV*. 3rd ed. Random House.

Parkinson, M. (2001). *The Times Graduate Job-hunting Guide*. Kogan Page.

 ## Websites

There are hundreds of recruitment websites, but the most useful websites for students and graduates are Trotman Publishing (www.trotmanpublishing.co.uk) and Prospects (www.prospects.csu.ac.uk). Trotman Publishing's site contains careers and higher education information and allows you to order books online. Prospects is an extensive careers website that enables you to explore different types of jobs and even to talk to graduates online. You can also use it to access the websites of individual companies, which will give you an idea of what they are looking for.

chapter 8

coping with stress

What is stress?

What is stress? It's that feeling of pressure, of wanting to escape, of being overwhelmed. It may bring physical symptoms like backache, or emotional reactions such as anger or weepiness.

There are many situations in life that bring on stress: being short of money; having to get out of lodgings; the ending of a relationship; reorganisation at work; drink, drug or eating problems. As a student, exams may be one of the more stressful situations you encounter, particularly if you have had a gap in studying.

Although most people experience stress at some time in their lives, not everyone reacts in the same way to the same situations. For instance, exams, interviews and deadlines are common causes of stress, yet some people thrive on the pressure, seeing them as a challenge. For them, a deadline or an event where they are put on the spot brings a rush of adrenaline. They are excited and know that if they push themselves they will succeed. In fact, for some people, a routine existence in which they know what they're going to

"57% of students feel under more stress than they did before starting their course."

Mori Student Living Survey, 2003

If you experience more than two or three of the symptoms listed below, you are probably suffering from stress.

- *sleeplessness*

- *change in eating habits*

- *increased intake of alcohol or drugs*

- *irritability*

- *persistent headache*

- *back pain with no physical cause*

- *lack of concentration*

- *tiredness*

- *forgetting and mislaying things*

- *inability to make decisions.*

be doing all day, every day can be as stressful as deadlines and exams are to others. So what does this tell us about stress? That very often it is not the event itself that is the problem, but the way we react to it.

When we feel very stressed it is often for one of two reasons – we feel we're not in control of our own lives, or we feel we're being judged and found wanting. That is why we often feel stressed when we are criticised. That is why exams can be so stressful – we are being judged and have no control over the matter. Of course the more important the outcome, the more stressful the situation is. A test in class where the marks don't count isn't nearly as stressful as doing finals.

Keys to dealing with stress

Getting yourself in control is the key to success in dealing with most stressful situations. To do this you need to gather as much information as possible about the situation and prepare for how to deal with it. This is true whether the event is an exam, an interview with your bank about your overdraft or a job reorganisation. Knowing what to expect, and having thought through in advance what you will say or do, will make you feel much more able to cope. So if there is something that you need to do about the situation, do it.

You will also need to get in control of yourself. Keep a check on internal dialogue, so that you stay positive. Watch out for your own patterns of behaviour that might be contributing to the stress. And when major stressful events happen, accept that this is part of life.

Coping with exams

First of all, find out what is involved well before the exams. Make sure you know in advance what you have to do, how many questions you have to answer and how many marks each question carries. If you have to do four questions carrying equal marks, you must complete all four questions and should allocate roughly the same amount of time to each. One of the most common mistakes people make is to spend so much time on the first question that they don't finish. If each question carries 25 marks and you only answer three you will have lost 25 marks immediately.

Top tips for revision

- *start early*

- *make a revision plan*

- *summarise, practise, actively memorise – don't just read*

- *use past exam papers*

- *build in relaxation time.*

Next, prepare. In this instance, preparation means revision. Start early. Make a revision plan based on how much work you need to do each week, not on how many hours you will spend. Do regular revision if you want to succeed – don't leave it all to the last minute and stay up all night cramming.

Your revision plan should consist of active learning, not just reading through. Active learning means doing practice questions, writing summary answers to questions, testing yourself on what you need to memorise, and thinking of different aspects of the topics you are covering. You've only done your revision when you know the work and can answer a question on it.

When you've made a plan, work out roughly how long the work you're going to do will take you per week. Be realistic. Build in breaks and regular relaxation time, preferably for doing something active like playing a sport, walking or cycling. Then make yourself a timetable. Allow some time for unexpected events that might stop you revising. It could only be catching a heavy cold, but you might find that for a few days you can't do much.

If you haven't done any exams for a while, it's a good idea to work through old exam papers in conditions similar to the actual exam. Start by preparing one question, and when you think you are reasonably sure of what you will write, do it to time, and go somewhere where you won't be interrupted, such as the library. Do it as you would in the exam, e.g. without looking up, unless that is allowed. Before you start, remember that this one doesn't matter –

it's a learning experience and by the time you actually do the exam you will be much better at it. As the exam draws nearer, gradually build up the number of questions you do in this way without a break. Most exams last three hours and you need to be able to concentrate for that period of time.

Monitor your plan so that you can see whether it is working. If you've been over-optimistic about how much work you can achieve, change it. A plan isn't a blueprint: it's your best guess of how the work will go. It's there to be changed. The important thing is to have a plan so that you know whether you are on track to get the work finished.

The night before the exam, have a relaxing evening and an early night. This may sound scary, but it pays off when you go into the exam room relaxed and clear-headed. Believe me, I've done it and it works! If you revise half the night before, you will go into the exam feeling tired and with everything going round in your head.

If you want more tips on coping with exams, there are plenty of books available, some of which are listed at the end of this chapter.

Coping with oral presentations

Speaking in public is one of the commonest fears. If you are not used to doing it, practising at college is the best way to get over stage fright. You will probably be given the opportunity to start by speaking to a small group without the teacher listening and gradually working up to presenting a paper to the class. If not, form your own group and practise on each other until you feel more comfortable.

It may help to share your fears with someone else. Often people are afraid they will dry up or they find the sight of other people looking at them unnerving. Take a step-by-step approach. For instance, if having people looking at you puts you off, ask them to look down the first time you do it so that you are not aware of all those eyes. Then let them look at you, but read from a paper. Next time, you will be ready to talk and look at your audience.

Give each other positive feedback on each improvement. You will find that you will soon be able to speak confidently to a group and eventually you will be able to do it without notes.

Life's little problems

Life has a habit of throwing up little problems and annoyances fairly regularly. They may be as simple as being late for a lecture because the bus didn't turn up or you got stuck in a traffic jam. For the most part, that kind of problem can be solved by leaving more time for the journey.

But there will always be some nuisance in life – getting stuck in a queue in the Post Office behind someone who seems to be having a long argument with the staff. Or forgetting to pay a bill and getting a nasty letter about it. Or someone picking a quarrel for no reason at all. Or going to see a particular band or performer and finding they've cancelled. Or having a washer go on a tap.

Sometimes we need to deal with the annoyance. For instance, if you miss the first part of a lecture, get the handouts and ask someone if you can see their notes. Check with the tutor to see if there is anything you should do to make up what you missed. If you've got a plumbing problem, deal with it yourself, get the plumber in, or phone the landlord.

At other times, there is nothing we can do but accept the situation and move on. Yet instead of that, we often spend a lot of time blaming ourselves or others: 'Why doesn't somebody do something about the traffic?' or 'I should have left more time.' We think we've been singled out for disappointment and dwell on it, making it into a much worse disappointment than it really was. It is as though we *want* to be miserable. We go over and over what happened, letting our thoughts dominate us instead of letting go. So someone was in a bad mood with you. Poor them, they must have been having a rotten day. So you missed your favourite band. Disappointing, but will it matter next week? You will be able to hear them another time.

Five **top tips** for coping with everyday problems

- decide what needs to be done

- do it straight away

- accept what you can't change

- put the problem behind you

- think positively.

How can you let go? By knowing that what is going through your head is just a thought. Every time you have a negative thought, stop. The world is just the same whether you have this thought or not. The only difference is how you feel. And how you feel is the result of the thoughts that are running through your head. It's your head, your brain. Nobody's making you think these thoughts.

Sometimes we keep running these thoughts through our heads because they are the way we explain our lives to ourselves. We say, 'I'm just unlucky – look, there's another example,' but we don't notice when small things go right. We notice when we have a long wait for the bus, but not when we catch one straight away.

Or we think, 'I'm not popular – nobody likes me,' when someone is bad-tempered with us. Yet it is just as likely that the person was annoyed about something quite different and was unaware of the effect they produced on us.

Or we say to ourselves, 'I'm no good at this. I always fail. There's no point in trying any more,' when other people have probably found things just as difficult, but have made a point of working at them and succeeding.

Repeating negative thoughts at every minor setback can become a habit and one that will pull you down. Some people cling to their excuses, so they don't have to bother. Don't be one of those. What do you want: to enjoy life and succeed, or to be miserable? Most people want to be happy as much of the time as possible and to be successful at what they are doing.

How does it serve you to dwell on the annoying things in life? It's your mind – you can think whatever thoughts you like. Turn your mind to the rest of the day. Think of something really good that is coming up. Get into the habit of dealing with small crises this way and you will find you are not nearly so stressed. If it helps to get something off your chest, tell someone. Then let it go.

Start a new 'life story'. Tell yourself you're one of those people who can put troubles behind them, who is prepared to keep going when things are difficult and who is as popular as the next person.

Life's big problems

Of course, not everything that happens in life is a small problem to be shrugged off. Some events have lasting consequences. If things don't turn out the way you hoped or expected, it can feel as though one setback has blighted your life. It is easy to fall into the trap of thinking that nothing like it has ever happened to anyone else.

This is because we don't generally learn about other people's struggles until we know them really well. And it's easy to make light of someone else's difficulties – and so much easier to solve their problems than our own! So look around you. Everyone has suffered setbacks of one kind or another and come through them.

You may even find that some of the events that seemed like disasters at the time turn out for the best. Sometimes this is because a better opportunity has come along that you would otherwise have missed out on. Sometimes the experience, though dark, transforms your life in a completely unexpected way. There is really no knowing what effect any one decision or event will have on the rest of your life.

Of course, sometimes problems are caused by something within us. If you keep finding yourself in the same difficult situation, there may be a pattern in your life that is caused by your own responses to people and events. This doesn't mean that you are to blame for what happens. On the contrary, we all have patterns in the way we respond to events, and this can be good as well as bad. Imagine having to work out how to deal with every event as it happened. Most of us respond in certain familiar ways and for the most part it works well enough.

When it doesn't work, recognising that fact is the first stage to dealing with it. You have choices. Accept that you can act differently. Know that unless you change what you are doing you will continue to get yourself in the same situation. Take it one step at a time. And if you have a serious problem, book an appointment with your student counsellor, or ring the college helpline if there is one.

Coping with stress

If you are going through a stressful time, whether it is because of exams coming up, money worries, relationship problems or anything else, now is the time to take care of yourself. When you are stressed your body needs all the help it can get so that it can cope with the effects of stress.

Top tips for when you're stressed

- eat a healthy diet
- get enough sleep
- exercise regularly
- build in relaxation time
- be kind to yourself.

The first thing to do if you are stressed is to make sure you have a healthy diet. Cut out burgers, chips, crisps, biscuits, cakes, sweets, chocolate, fizzy drinks and coffee. Cut down your alcohol consumption. Eat lots of vegetables, fresh fruit, fish and wholemeal bread, and drink plenty of water. If you want to snack, eat seeds or fruit. It may sound boring but it really does make a difference. Try it.

Make sure you get adequate sleep. Most people need seven or eight hours a night. If you have difficulty sleeping, do something relaxing before you go to bed. Ban late-night thrillers on television and anything that will tend to stimulate you. Try a milky drink before you go to bed, or a herbal tea such as camomile. Have a fixed bedtime routine.

This is a message to your system that it is time to go to sleep. If you are still tossing and turning, get up and do something for a while and then go back to bed.

When you are feeling stressed, there are a lot of stress hormones in your body. Help them to disperse by taking some vigorous exercise. It doesn't matter what it is: your favourite sport, a session in the gym or even a brisk walk will help. Exercise will also help you to sleep as long as you don't do it late at night.

Make sure you get enough relaxation time. Do something that you enjoy in a different environment that doesn't have stressful associations. Do it on a regular basis. It will take you out of yourself.

If you are feeling stressed, don't make matters worse by beating yourself up. Telling yourself, 'Nobody else is feeling like this,' or 'Nobody else has this problem – they're all enjoying themselves' won't help. The truth is that whatever has happened, great or small, is not unique. It may be that when you have a problem, your friends do not. We tend to notice this rather more than the times when someone else has a problem and our own lives are satisfactory.

Above all, know that it will pass. Nothing lasts for ever.

 ## Further reading

Evans, M. (2002) *Exams are Easy when you Know How*. How To Books.

Evans, M. (2003) *Make Exams Easy*. How To Books.

Hamilton, D. (2003) *Passing Exams: a guide for maximum success and minimum stress*. Continuum.

Naik, A. (2000). *The Little Book of Exam Calm: how to stay cool and still pass*. Hodder.

Simmons, R. (2002) *Stress*. Vega.

into action

So far you have read about how you can more effectively manage your life as a student. But no amount of reading in itself will enable you to manage your life. So now is the time to put ideas into action.

Setting goals

The best way to do this is to set yourself some goals, so that you can see whether you are achieving the targets you've set yourself. Goals have to be specific. 'I want to improve my grade from a C to a B on my next history assignment' is a goal. 'I want to improve my academic work' isn't, because it doesn't tell you in what way you want to improve it or by how much. It leaves it open to you to claim that you have achieved it by looking for any change that has happened. It also doesn't tell you when you have to do it. You can argue 'I will improve but I just haven't done it yet.'

 ## SMART goals

One way of ensuring that you set achievable goals is by using the SMART method. You may be familiar with it from school, or if you are a mature student, you may have used it at work.

A goal is SMART if it is:

Specific
Measurable
Achievable
Realistic
Time-bound.

The example above is SMART because it is **specific** – it tells you *exactly* what you have to do. It is **measurable** – it tells you that you have to improve by *one grade* – you will know when you get your assignment back if you have achieved it. It is **achievable** – it is possible in principle for someone to improve their work by one grade. Only you know whether it is **realistic** for you to do this on your next history assignment. It is **time-bound** – it tells you that you have to achieve it by the *next* assignment.

Exercise

Think of a goal that you would like to achieve. It doesn't have to be a major goal – in fact a small goal would be better. It doesn't have to relate to your academic work. It can be to do with paid work, or your social or domestic life. Write it down below and make notes against each of the SMART criteria.

Goal:

Specific

Measurable

Achievable

Realistic

Time-bound

Action plans

A goal tells you *what* you are going to achieve, but it doesn't tell you how to do it. To achieve your goals you need an action plan. A simple way of making an action plan is to answer the following questions:

- *What?*
- *Why?*
- *How?*
- *Who?*
- *Where?*
- *When?*

What? is your goal. *Why?* tells you what your motivation is for achieving it. The answer to *How?* will tell you what you have to do to achieve it. You will probably need to chunk down and set out a number of steps. (See Chapter 4 for more information about chunking.)

The answer to *Who?* will tell you who else is involved. (In some cases, of course, nobody but you will be involved.) *Where?* and *When?* will give you the place and the time for doing each step of the action plan. At each stage you need to be really specific.

An action plan might look like this:

What?   Improve my grade from a C to a B on my next history assignment

Why?   I want to get a better degree so that I can get a better job

How?   Increase my reading – read an additional five references

Who?   Me

Where? I will do the reading in my study bedroom

When?   I will get up at 8.00 a.m. each day and spend an extra hour reading before lectures start.

Of course I can't tell you whether this plan would improve your grade, because it depends on what your tutors advise you about your work. It is only an example of what an action plan might look like. Your action plan might look totally different.

Putting the plan into action

Having made your plan, the next and most important thing is to put it into action. In the previous example, you might want to set the alarm to ensure you got up by 8.00 a.m. each day and have the reading on your desk so that you are ready to make a start.

If you find moving from planning to action requires a lot of self-discipline, look back at Chapter 2 on motivation. Remind yourself of why you are *really* setting this goal. Maybe you're saying to yourself – improving my grade from C to B – who cares? But think to yourself what the difference in grade *really* means to you. That is why you are doing it.

Think back to what you found out about how to motivate yourself most effectively. Now is the time to put your methods into practice. Imagine that you could get what you *really* want, if you just get up at 8.00 a.m. each day and do the reading – or whatever it is you need to do. Would you do it? Because if you really want something, the effort is worthwhile. So keep reminding yourself of what you *really* want and how achieving your goal will help you get it.

"There is a close correlation between getting up in the morning and getting on in the world."

Ron Dentinger

Sticking to the plan

Are you a starter or a finisher? Some people find it hard to start things but once going, they stick to the plan. Other people enjoy starting something new but get bored when the novelty wears off.

If you find it hard to start, think of what would make it easier for you to get going. Think back to a time when you did something new. How did you do it? What made it go well? Maybe it was the reason *why* you were doing it, or *how* or *when* you did it. Think about it and experiment if necessary. Knowing how to kick-start yourself is a useful skill which will stand you in good stead throughout your studies and beyond.

Top tips for sticking to a plan

- *before you stop work, write down your plan for the next day*

- *do the things you have listed early in the day*

- *monitor your progress*

- *reward yourself for success*

- *remind yourself of why you are really doing it.*

If you are a starter who doesn't always stay the course, think of what it would take to keep you going. Imagine that each time you do something it is for the first time. Think of that feeling of starting something new, and maybe tackle the task you have set yourself in a slightly different way each time.

Another way is to think of a time when you are mainly acting out of habit, for instance, getting up in the morning and getting ready for the day. Fit what you want to do into that routine. As you are in a routine anyway, adding one more thing to what you do may be easier than doing it at some other time. Find out what works for you.

Whatever you do, keep a note of what you have done – put it in your timetable, diary or calendar. If the mere thought of keeping any kind of record puts you off, just put a tick. Monitoring is one of the best ways of keeping on track. You will know that you are sticking to the plan and that in itself will make you feel good. And you will find that there is some part of you that is looking for the tick. Give yourself a reward each time you tick off something you have done.

Some people like to work with someone else who is doing the same thing so that they can keep each other up to scratch. The knowledge that you are going to have to tell someone else how you are doing often acts as a spur. If you do this, make sure your chosen buddy is committed to succeeding and has a positive frame of mind. If you buddy up with someone who moans about why they can't do it, or never sticks to their intentions, they will only make it harder for you.

 ## Is the plan working?

Of course there is no point in sticking to a plan if it doesn't get results. In the example above, did the extra reading result in an improved grade? If not, then you need to change the plan. A plan is just a tool. If it doesn't do the job, change it.

By checking whether your plan is working you will also learn something about how to make a good plan and how you can succeed. After a few times you will become good at making a plan that will work for you and that you can stick to.

 ## Reflect – plan – act – review

Another way of looking at the process outlined in this chapter is shown below. You begin by reflecting on what you want to do. Then you create a detailed plan, and put it into action. Lastly you review it, to see how well it is working. If it isn't as successful as you would like, you reflect on why, and what would work better. Then you create a new plan. You can go round this cycle as many times as you need to.

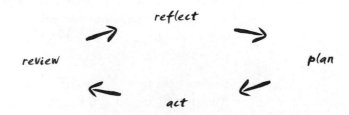

Aiming in the right direction

So far we have looked at short-term goals. You can have long-term goals as well, but of course you won't have a detailed action plan to cover your whole journey. You may have a short-term action plan to get you started, but as you go along you will have to take decisions further down the line as you find out more about your long-term goals.

One of the most powerful things you can do is write down your ultimate goal and the date you expect to achieve it, with an outline of how you intend to get there.

Famously, Michael Heseltine, a leading Tory politician in the 1980s and 1990s, wrote an outline of his career on the back of an envelope when he was still at university. It finished with, '1990s – 10 Downing Street'. Although he never actually made it to Number 10, he became Deputy Prime Minister in the 1990s – which was pretty close to his original goal.

Of course your aims are probably more modest than becoming Prime Minister. They may not relate to careers or earning money. Whatever it is that you *really* want, write it down. You don't have to show it to anyone. The person to whom you are making a commitment is you. Write down what you *really* want and acknowledge it to yourself. This may feel like an act of courage.

There is a story that in the 1950s a group of students at Yale University were asked if they had written down any goals or made any plans. Only 3% of the entire group had done so.

Twenty-five years later, the members of the group were contacted again and each was asked how satisfied they were with their lives.

The 3% who had written down their goals were happier and more satisfied than the rest of their former classmates. And they earned more than the remaining 97% put together.

Mental preparation

One of the reasons why we sometimes fail to carry out our intentions is because we are not mentally prepared. We say, 'I can't see myself doing that'. To overcome this, sportsmen and women spend time in mental preparation, visualising success, before they compete.

What works for them will work for you. Visualise yourself taking the necessary steps and achieving your goal. It doesn't matter if you think you can visualise or not. Imagining doing it will bring it nearer. Think about how it will be when you have achieved what you want. Build up the picture in your own mind. Maybe you want to concentrate on hearing what people will say to you or how you will feel. Do whatever works for you. Then go into action.

"If you think you can, or you think you can't, you're probably right."

Henry Ford

So prepare yourself for carrying out your plan and give yourself the best chance to succeed. Accept whatever happens and learn from it. If it doesn't work out the way you intended, you will know better next time. Learning is about the opportunity to make mistakes.

There is a saying, 'The person who never made a mistake never made anything.' When you do something new or different, you won't know exactly how best to do it. You only get that knowledge with experience. Instead of worrying or blaming yourself if everything doesn't go quite according to plan, just notice what happens.

So say to yourself, 'That was interesting – I didn't think it would turn out that way. Now let's see what happens when I do it a different way.' Imagine you are conducting an experiment. You don't know whether your plan will work, but you are testing it out in the best conditions possible. You will soon have a plan that works for you – one that you can rely on.

What if you don't know what you want?

Some of you reading this will find that the goals and action plans you have set out are too far removed from what really motivates you. Or you may have found the exercise difficult because you don't have specific goals in mind. Your aims may be more to do with your own personal development than with any specific career or academic goal.

This is sometimes the case with mature students. If you are a mature student you may have a strong but hard-to-define feeling that you can do more with your life than you have so far, that you are capable of more, are worth more.

If this is true of you, you may find it difficult to write down SMART goals and action plans for what you *really* want. If your motivation for doing the course is finding out what you are capable of or remedying a feeling of lack in your life, you won't be able to turn that into SMART goals and action plans.

This doesn't mean that they are not relevant to you, as there will be many times when you have short-term goals to achieve, but you will need another way of keeping track of your general progress and checking that you are going in the right direction. One very good way of doing this is to keep a journal in which you record your thoughts, your hopes and fears, your successes and failures.

Some academic courses with a strong personal development theme include a journal element. If you are interested in this idea, look through the course literature or ask your tutors. Bear in mind that these journals may be assessed, although you probably won't have to share them with anybody except your tutor.

But you don't have to do a journal as part of your course. You can do it just as well for yourself. In fact there may be advantages in doing it just for yourself as it means you can do it however you like.

Questions to ask yourself when you start a journal

- What's really important to you? And why is it important?

- Who do you most admire? And why?

- If you could achieve any one thing in your life, what would it be?

- If you could spend a day however you liked, how would you spend it?

- If you could change one thing about yourself, what would it be?

The best way of keeping a journal is to set aside a regular time, daily or weekly, to write it up. Be honest with yourself, and keep it safe from other people's eyes if you don't want to share it.

One of the most important ways of gaining from your journal is to set aside some time, perhaps once a month, to look through your previous entries. You will be amazed at how you have progressed. It seems to be part of human nature to forget the things we used to find difficult. We often value what we can't do, but take for granted what we can do.

Set aside some time to write down in your journal what has changed for you in the last month. You might like to keep this note in a separate place as a record of how you are changing. It will provide the proof that you really are finding out what you are capable of. And later on, when you begin looking for jobs, you may find that you can draw on it to show how you have solved problems and overcome difficulties.

Confidence building

Keeping a journal will build your confidence in yourself and your achievements, great or small. All too often, students put themselves down or disregard their strengths. This characteristic isn't very helpful in life or very attractive. Of course, bragging isn't attractive either. Often when people brag it's because they are covering up their underlying lack of confidence. So cultivate a balanced view of yourself, your strengths and weaknesses. This will help you to achieve whatever you want in life.

What stops us recognising our own strengths is often fear: fear of being judged; fear of failure; and fear of success.

To deal with fear of being judged, think of specific examples. For instance, if you know you stand by your friends, think of a time when you did just that when it would have been easier not to. If you are good at sport, think of a time when you helped your team to win. If you stick at things even when they are difficult, think of a specific time when you did that.

To deal with fear of failure, recognise that owning a strength doesn't mean that you have to succeed 100% every single time. Everyone has off days. Just know that, generally speaking, that is how you behave and what you are able to do. If you want to develop your abilities, be prepared to fail before you succeed. You weren't born being able to do everything you can do now. The first time you tried to walk you fell over. As a baby you had the

Questions to ask yourself regularly in your journal

- *What are you most pleased about today/this week?*

- *What does this tell you about yourself?*

- *What would you like to have done differently?*

- *How will you handle a similar situation next time?*

"The greatest mistake you can make in life is to be continually fearing that you will make one."

Elbert Hubbard

wisdom to get up and try again until you could do it. So make a friend of failure, because it leads you to success.

Fear of success is perhaps the hardest to cope with. Sometimes claiming that we are good at something feels as though we are talking about someone else. Is that really me I am talking about? This person who is good at negotiating with other people in the group, or who has lots of good ideas, or who is hard working? Start noticing what you can do and when and how you do it. Then you will begin to feel that you own your skills or qualities and you will feel comfortable acknowledging them.

To help you start building up your confidence in your own abilities, work with a friend who knows you well. Identify each other's strengths and examples of them. It is often easier to be objective about somebody else. If you find it hard to do this, think of two other people – any two people will do. Then think of how your friend shares a strength with one of them but not the other. Choose another two people and do the same thing. You will soon generate a list.

You can also do this on your own to come up with a list of your own strengths. Remember that you are looking for positive qualities. It doesn't matter what you come up with. Just write down whatever comes into your head. You can refine it later.

Look at your list regularly. Compare it with what you learn from your journal. Notice how you are changing and improving. If you don't like writing, you can do this without using the journal method. Keep a log of what you have achieved instead. Make it specific and date it. Any time you are feeling unsure of yourself, read it through.

chapter 10

help yourself

**This chapter
shows you how
to:**

• **know your own
strengths and
weaknesses**

• **draw on support
from other
people around you**

• **make the most of
your
circumstances**

• **be positive**

• **use the techniques
in this book**

• **find out about
the professional
support available
in your university.**

During your time at university you will face a number of challenges. To meet them successfully you will need to make the most of what you have got going for you, whether this is to do with your own strengths or the support of other people.

Know yourself

The most important starting point is to know yourself – your strengths and weaknesses, how you react to situations, what triggers off your behaviour and what helps you to succeed.

Make a list of the strengths you have that will help you to make the most of university. Use the checklist below to start you thinking or make your own list. If you have used the journal method or other techniques described in Chapter 9, look back at what you have written and note what is relevant.

Of course you may have quite different qualities on your list. What is important is that what you have written down is true of you, and will help you to get the best out of your studies. Remind yourself of your strengths often, and particularly when you hit a bad patch. Tell yourself, 'I am a positive person and I have got a sense of proportion,' or whatever qualities you have come up with. Own your strengths. Make them work for you.

Now think about your weaknesses. In connection with your studies, what one thing would you like to change about yourself that would make you more successful and enjoy your course more?

Strengths

act on ideas	adaptable	ambitious
analytical	assertive	careful
competitive	courageous	creative
decisive	dynamic	enthusiastic
friendly	hard working	imaginative
know when to let go	optimistic	persevering
popular	positive	realistic
reliable	resolute	self-aware
sense of humour	sense of proportion	support others
understand other people	willing	

You may have thought of something like 'too often taking a back seat', or 'losing my temper', or 'not having enough faith in myself'. Whatever it is, you can change it if you want to. Start by becoming more aware of when you do it. Think back to any situation when you did this – took a back seat or lost your temper or whatever it was. Replay it in your mind. What triggered it off? Knowing this is the first stage to being able to change your behaviour.

If you keep taking a back seat – for example, not speaking up in a group – ask yourself, 'What would happen if I did speak up?' You may find all sorts of fears come to light. But are they really likely to come true? Letting them see the light of day often makes them seem less important.

If you find yourself losing your temper, be aware of what is going on inside your head. Are you imagining that the other person is thinking bad thoughts about you? How do you know? They may not be thinking anything of the kind. Learn the difference between your own imaginings and what is actually happening. The other person might be very surprised if they knew what you were thinking about them.

If your first reaction to anything new is to think, 'I couldn't do that,' think about all the new things you have done in your life. Everything that you can do now, you had to do for the first time. If you never had the confidence to do something new, you would never have learnt to walk or talk or pass exams or ride a bike or boil an egg.

These are only examples, and you have probably put down something quite different. The important thing is to get to know yourself and what works for you in managing your own life. Pay attention to your own behaviour and what happens inside your head. Also listen to people you trust. If they tell you something about yourself, think about it. It may well be true.

Then start by changing your behaviour in a small and unthreatening way. Do it bit by bit and you will gradually find that your behaviour becomes more positive.

Support from other people

People who support you are worth their weight in gold. If you have a supportive partner, family or friends, let them know that you value their support and don't take them for granted. Be aware of just what support they are giving you. This may be moral support, such as encouraging you to keep going and persuading you that you can succeed, or urging you on to do something about a situation you find hard to tackle. They may just be there to listen to you when you need someone to take your part. Or there may be people in your life who help you in practical ways – over money, for example, or by doing things for you, such as giving you lifts or doing the chores.

If the people closest to you are not as supportive as you would like, think about what would make the most difference to your life. Be prepared to ask – if you don't ask, you don't get. Explain to them what you need from them and what it means to you. Be specific. Tell them *exactly* what it is you need. This might be time without interruptions when you are working on an assignment, or jobs such as shopping. If your partner or family will gain a long-term advantage from you succeeding at your studies, remind them – gently! But recognise that they have needs too. When they are supportive, thank them and let them know you appreciate what they are doing. Think what you could do for them in exchange, so that it's not all one way.

If you are asking for help from your parents, it may seem that there's nothing much you can do in return. But perhaps there is. Ask them. That way everybody wins. Maybe they just want you to succeed, so work hard. Maybe there's something you can do at another time, during the holidays for example, like keeping your room tidy. The same applies to your partner. What they want from you in return may be something you've never thought of, so ask them.

Think about the people you hang out with. Do they support you and do you support them? If the answer is yes, this could be a big plus in your life. If the answer is no, think seriously about whether you have the right friends. If you don't support each other in what you want to do, what kind of friends are they?

Sometimes students find that they don't make close friends at university to start with. This may happen because they are on a modular course where they don't stay with the same group for very long, or because they are mature students in a mainly 18-year-old group, international students or first-years living off campus.

If this is you, make a point of joining groups that will bring you into contact with other students in the same boat. Be prepared to make the first move. There will be plenty of people who want to make friends. When things get tough you will be glad that there are other people who will support you.

Making the most of your circumstances

A good way of helping you to make the most of your circumstances is to list the key issues under 'helps' and 'hindrances'.

One way of doing this is to follow the example below:

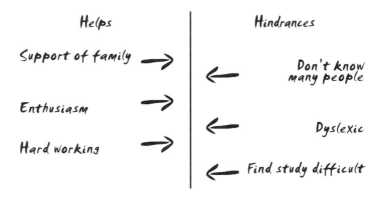

Do your own helps and hindrances diagram before reading on. Draw long arrows for the most important helps and hindrances and short ones for the least important.

Now, for each hindrance, think of a way you can minimise it.

Taking the example above, for instance, if you don't know many people, join a group or society. If you are dyslexic, make sure you get all the help you are entitled to. Your university will have some arrangements for assessing you and providing you with support. If you find study difficult, take advantage of any study skills courses that are being run. Or combine some of these things. Get together with other people in your group who are having study problems and work together. That way you can overcome your study skills problems and get to know more people at the same time.

At the time, you may have found that you had enough to do, getting to know where the lecture rooms were and getting to know people. Often students become overloaded with information and it goes in one ear and out the other. This is a pity because sooner or later you will probably need some of the information you were given.

If you are reading this before you go to university, get yourself a box, put all the stuff into it that you are given at induction, and label it. This material should include the university handbook, leaflets on university services and courses, and anything at all that looks a bit official. One day you will need it, so keep it all together. When you want advice or help, look through the box. You may be surprised to find just what services your university offers.

Check to see which of these your university offers services or information on:

- *accommodation*
- *careers*
- *chaplaincy – variety of faiths*
- *children*
- *computers*
- *counselling*
- *disabilities*
- *dyslexia*
- *finance*
- *health*
- *international*
- *jobshop*
- *languages*
- *legal*
- *mentoring*

If you have lost all the material or don't know where it is, look through the checklist to get an idea of the range of services your university might offer. Bear in mind that not every university offers the same services. Most services are run by the university itself, but some may be run by the students' union.

Face-to-face guidance services may be available on a drop-in basis, or you may have to make an appointment. In some cases you may find that you can get what you need from information leaflets. Some services may be available on-line. There is a list of useful websites at the end of this chapter.

Look at the university website for information, or ask around. You can try asking your tutor. If you have a personal tutor in your first year they are more likely to be clued up than other tutors. If there is a departmental secretary, ask them – they will probably be able to find out for you even if they don't know. Ask someone in the students' union. Ask in the library – they might have leaflets about other services. Ask in the careers service – they may have links to other services or be aware of them. Phone the switchboard. Keep asking until you get a result, because very likely the support you want is there.

Useful websites

- *nightline (night-time listening and information service)*
- *nursery*
- *personal development activities*
- *personal safety*
- *sports and leisure*
- *students' rights*
- *study skills*
- *welfare.*

www.dfes.gov.uk/student support
Information on financial support for part-time students, students with children, students with disabilities, mature students.

www.hero.ac.uk – click on 'guidance and support'
Information and guidance on: academic matters; health; safety and security; cultural support for women, international students, mature students and students from ethnic minorities; disabled students; students with children.

www.nightline.niss.ac.uk
Information and guidance on money, travel, crime, sexuality, sexual health, general health, jobs, legal. Nightline phone numbers for individual universities.

www.nusline.co.uk
Information and guidance on housing, health, head stuff, drugs, education, disabilities, money, freshers, sex, discount listings. Links to local students' union websites, giving information on local discounts, events, job placements.

www.studentUK.com
Information and guidance on drugs, study, accommodation, money, sex, jobs, health, safety, travel.

www.support4learning.org.uk
Information and guidance on community – accommodation, childcare, legal resources etc. – careers, job search, education, money, health, counselling.

www.uniserve.com
Information and guidance on academic matters, accommodation, careers, entertainment, health and sex, money, travel.

A website designed for students by students.

A final word

University can be a great experience, so:

- make plenty of friends

- become all that you are capable of

- have fun!